BEFORE YOU JUDGE ME

BEING DAVID

BEFORE YOU JUDGE ME

BEING DAVID

David Oldfield

First published in 2019 by New Holland Publishers
London • Sydney • Auckland

Bentinck House, 3–8 Bolsover Street, London W1W 5BB, UK
1/66 Gibbes Street, Chatswood, NSW 2067, Australia
5/39 Woodside Ave, Northcote, Auckland 0627, New Zealand

newhollandpublishers.com

A record of this book is held at the British Library and the National Library of Australia.

ISBN 9781921024818

Group Managing Director: Fiona Schultz
Publisher: Fiona Schultz
Project Editor: Liz Hardy
Designer: Andrew Davies
Production Director: Arlene Gippert
Printer: Toppan Leefung Printing Limited

10 9 8 7 6 5 4 3 2 1

Keep up with New Holland Publishers on Facebook
facebook.com/NewHollandPublishers

Contents

Preface

There are no mysteries; everything can be explained logically and rationally. Those matters that seem mysterious are either yet to be explained or the explanation already on offer doesn't suit people. The truth needs life breathed into it because time has a tendency to erase the truth, while lies seemingly have a life of their own. I've beaten a lot of people in my life and stood up to many more, and people you've beaten or stood against generally don't remember you fondly, fairly or honestly, so don't ever be surprised by what they say.

I always tell my sons to never be afraid of anything, but to always be careful of everything. It's something I wish I'd learned as a child, because whilst there wasn't ever very much I was afraid of, I was also not very careful with anything; in fact, I probably wasn't careful at all.

How well I remember my desperate attempts to make nitroglycerine – yes, you're reading the life of a crazy guy. I was eleven at the time and fortunately I always failed; I just couldn't quite get the bicarbonate of soda wash right. I blew myself up a couple times as a child, but fortunately not to the extent I would have, had I gotten that wash right for the nitro, but I'll get to that later.

From the outset, I need to tell you that my faults are unrelated to my parents – I had the most wonderful dad and mum and I was fortunate beyond belief to have been their son. It's likely the case that at least some of what I see that's bad in me will naturally surface in my own sons, and I can already see some of that in my youngest son, and I don't like it. At this stage, my eldest son seems to take more after my wife, and I don't like that much either, but he says he wants to be like his dad – no accounting for taste? There are aspects of my personality I don't want my children to emulate and others where I'd like them to be like me, except much better.

There were perhaps experiences in my childhood that were different and certainly, we are all very much products of our environment, or at least greatly influenced by it, and in that, I was lucky that my parents were unusually fair, extraordinarily honest people and immensely popular with all who knew them. While we can explore how I turned out the way I did, I like to think my parents were only responsible for what's good about me – something else gave me my faults, and believe me, I know all those faults intimately.

Of course I know there were things in my childhood that shaped me in certain ways and my parents have a level of responsibility for that, but to accept that on its own lays blame at their feet and they were fine people deserving of much better thoughts. In the end, we make our own choices and we must learn from the results of those choices however good or bad they may be. When we have our own children we will need to know our mistakes so as to have a chance to save our kids from the same poor decisions.

In fairness to myself, much of what my detractors say about me isn't at all accurate – much of it is merely unfair and without context and stems from the simple human character failing of wanting to do whatever one can to drag down what they don't like, fear, disagree with or just simply don't understand. Most people seem to get that the world isn't a fair place, but I'm not sure if, as a group, we acknowledge that is the case, mostly because people are often biased and unfair in their judgements. Often, they go on mistaken impressions, somebody else's information or a desire to believe the worst about someone without questioning motives for what is reported.

It is said there is no such thing as a second first impression, and how true that is – something that at times has had an impact on me that wasn't helpful. When I was very young, a lot of that would have been because I was really quite shy and not very outgoing and that never makes a good first impression, if much of an impression at all.

As ridiculous as it may seem to some, that shy little boy still influences me and perhaps that has led to some of the way I've been perceived at times.

I was, however, adventurous and dangerous to a degree that these days, even I find surprising when I think back on things. Truth be known, I'm still a risk taker but maybe the risks are a little more calculated these days.

This isn't just a look at why I am as I am and perhaps how that came about, but also a study of human behaviour and interactions. On many levels, it might very well be about you, because for the most part, it's what we've seen and experienced in life that makes us who we are and, sometimes, who we're not.

Sure, there is the matter of genes, and I can see so much of my parents in me – in the way I look and in personality traits as well. I have my mother's eyes, my father's build and my skin and hair is virtually a cross between the two of them. But how much of my personality did I inherit and how much developed through the environment of being with my parents and what I observed and subconsciously and consciously learned from them and those around me and the times in which I lived?

Personally, I lean mostly towards environment. I'm very much of the view we're largely products of our environment. That wouldn't suit a lot of people, especially those wanting to find genetic markers to explain their individual circumstances, as they see them.

I was going to say that it's the negative traits that one notices, but that's not right, it's just they stand out when looking for problems and I tend to focus on the problems. In some respects, it's one of the negative things I see about myself, I tend to focus on what's bad and not what's good. I always see the bad first and I acknowledge that may sometimes inhibit me from seeing the good, if there is any. I kind of figure the good takes care of itself, but the evil needs to be rooted out. If you're looking for a person who identifies problems and finds solutions, I'm your man, but I know not seeing good in equal proportion makes me a lot sadder than I could be and that's not great for my health, or the way others see me.

If you have an open mind you're very rare; but if you do, then reading what is ahead will explain almost everything about me, people I've met, many of whom you'll be aware of, and, I expect you'll see something of yourself as well.

Being David: Early Family Life

I always respected and admired David's passion and dedication to his family, a family that shaped his views and values. He wore his father's suffering from the war deep in his heart and his mother's passion for life on his sleeve.

– The Honourable Bob Baldwin MP,
former parliamentary secretary (assistant minister) and
Member for Paterson,
March 2018

I suppose I could start with the usual of where I was born and so on and to a degree that's a part of the story, but it's a time over which you have no control or memory of. In reality, these are matters you are aware of through others – family, friends, and often just photographs.

Photographs are interesting. I meet so many people who tell me about the things they remember as a child, the experiences they had, and yet for the most part, these are not their memories as such, but the memories of others and sometimes a memory they manifest due to a photograph they have. Adults genuinely remember little if anything before the age of three to four and for a range of reasons some will have difficulty remembering much of their lives before five or six, or even later. There are specific events that may be imprinted in our minds, things we clearly visualise, but for the most part, our early memories, if they're still there, are not terribly accessible. When an adult tells you about something they remember as a baby or perhaps as a toddler, they're not having you on, but they are having themselves on

– they likely genuinely believe they remember, but chances are what they really remember is a story about themselves that someone told them later in life.

I only note this in the sense that there are so many things we think we know about ourselves that we really don't. Sometimes, even the memories we think are ours aren't ours at all, though the experiences those memories tell of may very well have been ours, and no doubt they shaped us, even if only in a small way.

I can very clearly see what I consider to be the first time I kissed a girl – maybe I had done it earlier, but there is a specific experience that I can see in my mind like a movie playing. Her name was Sally, she had a short blonde bob and it happened in the sandpit of my preschool in Condamine Street Balgowlah. Don't go looking for the scene of this remarkable moment in history – today, it's a car park and where David met Sally, is now asphalt. I used to mark this event as having happened when I was six years old, but writing this now, I realise I was four or slightly less, because I know I didn't go to that kindergarten after four years of age.

So was that the first time I kissed a girl or just the first time I remember? We'll never know, though I know for sure the last time I kissed a girl and there'll be no more of that for me – I'm done with women. Just kidding. Can't live with them, but willing to try! Sorry more kidding around. I've often thought I'd happily be gay – you know, men together, doing things men do, adventure and fun without all the drama we allow women to bring into our lives – then I get to the sex part of all that and the prospect of being gay goes right out the window. I'm strongly of the view that a person's sexuality is entirely their business – anything that floats your boat, however much of a freaky weirdo you might be, is entirely your business not mine, and good luck to you provided it's all between consenting adults!

I was born to parents who even now, many years after their deaths, I'm still trying to understand. Perhaps make that, wanting to understand so much more, to know so much more.

My parents had both been married before and back in those days divorce took a while so some plans got put on hold – I was one of those plans. Mum and Dad met the old-fashioned way, or in more traditional circumstances – they met at work. My mum's name was June and my dad, the always very cheeky Bill Oldfield, when mum was introduced as June, said to her, 'I was born in June.'

These days I imagine that would be some kind of sexual harassment in the workplace and my mother would be tweeting herself as involved with #MeToo. It was the early 1950s and clearly she didn't take it badly as they soon after started dating. They were engaged and eventually living together and I suppose that was in sin at that time, but Dad's divorce from his first wife hadn't been finalised and that's why I was on hold. My dad desperately wanted a son, but neither of them was willing to do that while they were unmarried – call them old-fashioned. Dad's divorce finally came through, he and Mum got married and the quest for a son got under way. Dad is said to have readily told people he was having a son and that, 'I put my order in last night.'

My parents always said I was the longest pregnancy on record as it was fifteen months from when dad started 'putting in his order' until I appeared, as desired, a bouncing baby boy.

> Bill was oh so proud of David – he regaled us with all the things David was going to do.
>
> – Betty Brookes,
> June Oldfield's last surviving friend,
> May 2018

For some context, Mum turned thirty-five the year I was born, and Dad had turned forty just two weeks before I was born, in 1958. That was relatively old to become parents for the first time, except it wasn't the first time for either of them. It was, however, a long time between drinks. Dad had married during World War II and late in the war, when he was considered 'missing presumed dead', his then wife took the worst to be the case and thought herself a widow. Whatever happened between them, his return some weeks after Japan surrendered in 1945 didn't make for much in the way of a reconciliation and he moved from Perth to Sydney.

Mum had also married during World War II and, sadly, her husband returned from combat a damaged man who turned to alcohol and soon after became a violent and abusive husband. My mum, at twenty-four years of age, took her daughter and son, both under three years of age, and left him. She asked for nothing in the divorce, not even any form of child support; she didn't want her alcoholic husband to have any hold over the children.

I never knew my mum's first husband. I heard about him and I learned of his war record and I can't help but feel sorry for him – he saw a lot of ugly things while in combat and the fact is, some dealt with it better than others. There is more help for such issues now than there ever was in 1945.

My father's daughter from his first marriage, Lesley, lived with his ex-wife in Perth. I didn't see a lot of her. I met her for the first time when she was eighteen and I was four. Just like kissing Sally, I have that memory stored like a film. I can picture the drive over to pick Lesley up and the hotel in which she was staying, but I don't remember much of her beyond that. For the most part, our lives have been entirely separate.

My dad adopted my mum's two children, Carolyn and Wayne, and we all lived together, but they were much older than me, so by the time I was three, they'd both moved out of home. My brother had joined the air force as an apprentice and became an electrical engineer while my sister was a secretary and was flatting with a couple of her girlfriends.

I referred to them as my brother and sister because that was how I saw them, on the occasions I did see them. My brother was stationed at Richmond and later at Wagga Wagga and my sister was amazingly popular and enormously busy. It wasn't until I was well into my teens that I had any idea that while Wayne and Carolyn were brother and sister, I was only their half-brother, and ultimately having that information didn't alter the way I viewed them.

People back then carried something akin to shame at having been previously married, I don't know if that's why I was never told the nature of our household make-up or whether no-one thought I needed to know. We didn't look that much alike except that we all had dark brown eyes, dark brown hair and olive skin courtesy of my mother, but I wasn't quite as dark as Mum, Carolyn and Wayne, and I was physically different because of my dad's influence.

I wish I'd gotten my dad's blue eyes, but at least my son Henry has them – lucky boy. I often see my dad when I look into Henry's eyes and as a newborn, Henry looked so much like my dad it was as if it was him.

I'm very proud of Wayne and Carolyn, though I tend to think they kind of tolerated me. It must be difficult to be out-and-about eighteen and nineteen-year-olds and have a brother in preschool.

Also, in the case of my brother, I inadvertently changed his life by simply being born. Dad had been the father he so wanted and had been in that role for years, but then I came along, and that relationship changed. As soon as I was walking, my mother became concerned Wayne's beloved dog, Kim, would knock me over, so poor Kim had to go. In this way, I was held responsible for Wayne losing his dog. By the time I was a bit over two, I'd taken his dad and his dog – it wasn't a great start to brotherly love. Still, I didn't know these things and my brother wasn't around except on the occasional weekend.

As a regular, he volunteered for Vietnam and did his tour in 1968–69, and just before that he spent three months in New Guinea for jungle training. It was a tense time in the Oldfield home as mum worried about Wayne getting wounded or killed in action. I don't recollect being worried. I wasn't up on the notion people I knew would die; I suppose I thought it was people I didn't know who died.

I can't remember how Dad saw it. My dad was always very stoic and by that time he was fifty, so to me at ten he seemed old and wise and tough as nails. I suspect he was concerned for Wayne but he never seemed a very emotional man – or not so that it showed. I don't remember ever seeing my dad cry. That may have been something men of his generation just didn't do.

You'd fairly describe my dad as old school. He was born towards the end of WW I and was a teenager in the Great Depression. He'd had a hard, old-time traditional sort of life. He left school at fourteen and went to work, an especially difficult thing in Australia in 1932.

My dad's Christian name is Ernest, but when he started work, the boss said, 'We've already got an Ernest, so we're going to call you Bill.' Just like that, his named was changed for him and he was 'Bill' for the rest of his life. He even used to get mail addressed to W. Oldfield because many assumed his name was William.

By the time he was sixteen, 'Bill' was essentially the company's accountant. You couldn't do that today – leave school at fourteen and be in charge of the accounts at sixteen – but Dad had a head for figures and fourteen-year-olds then were completely different to fourteen-year-olds today.

In 1939, at twenty-one, Dad volunteered for WW II. He joined the army and in 1940 he transferred to the air force. He trained as an air gunner wireless operator and was assigned to 2 Squadron, a unit flying Hudson light bombers. He was on duty at the RAAF airfield during the bombing of Darwin and weeks later, the last man on the last plane out of Ambon before the Japanese overran the island. He flew seventy-eight combat missions, was decorated for bravery with a DFM and PUC, commissioned from the ranks and made Western and North Western Area Gunnery Leader.

He lost virtually all of his original friends. His best mate, Isaac Reed, was beheaded by the Japanese in February 1942, and by 1943, Dad was the only original air gunner of the squadron who was still alive. While flying as an observer in a B24 Liberator bomber late in the war, he was shot down and taken prisoner under fire.

He'd fought a hell of a war my dad. Many called him a hero but he never thought of himself that way, not even close. Dad didn't talk about the war, though I remember we weren't allowed anything in the house that was made in Japan, until the time came when that was impossible because so much was made in Japan and no longer in Australia.

Mum's good friend Betty told me that she and her husband were at my parents' place for dinner around 1956 when Dad happened to notice 'made in Japan' on the underside of his coffee cup. He immediately smashed it on the table and got Betty's husband Bobby to help him remove all the rest of the crockery from the table and get rid of it.

It would be very difficult for Australians today to understand the hatred of the Japanese that was left over from WW II. I suspect many people could never excuse the way my dad was about such things, but that'll be because they are people of this time and unable to picture his world. Most of my dad's mates, including his best mate, were killed in the war. A lot of them weren't killed in action, but murdered as prisoners of war.

Dad himself suffered indescribably as a prisoner of war – beaten, interrogated, tortured, starved. His experiences and knowledge of the crimes of the Japanese were such that in 1946 he was called to give evidence to the United Nations War Crimes Commission.

In the 1990s, he told me of a recurring dream that stayed with him for more than twenty years after the war. He'd invited his interrogators/torturers to dinner and they all had a nice time. All seemed forgiven, and then when dinner was over, he killed them and buried them in our backyard.

Dad eventually managed to put the atrocities of the war behind him. In the late 1980s, he told me he'd forgiven his captors, but he said he would never be able to trust them. He did a great deal to help a Japanese friend of mine, Kyoichi, so clearly he didn't carry his thoughts over to the generations of Japanese not directly involved in the war.

One of the thousands of things I never asked my dad and often kick myself about, was, 'What was it like for you when Wayne was in Vietnam? What were you thinking?' I suspect he would have comforted my mum, but never let on about his own concerns for fear of worrying her even further. When Wayne came back, I remember going out to the airport when he arrived in Australia. The waiting is a blur, but I remember seeing him suddenly emerge – I can see him in his uniform and dark blue beret and I remember my mum's tears of joy.

I can't much understand what Vietnam was like for him. He was a bit messed up. I think they all likely were to one degree or another, but Wayne seemed okay – looking back, maybe a little angry or aggressive. It's understandable; he'd fought a war without being appreciated. It's awful how Vietnam veterans were treated for decades afterwards – truly a dark time in Australia's history and I still haven't forgiven those responsible, nor will I. One of the very clear memories I do have of the early 1970s were the grubs who screamed at my brother's ilk that they were murderers, baby killers. It affected me so God knows the effect it truly had on him.

In my twenties, I once said to Wayne, 'I don't understand. Dad had six years of war, his best mates were killed, he was captured, beaten, tortured nearly killed dozens of times and he's okay. You were gone for a year and you're a mess?'

My brother just said, 'They were tougher than we were.' And that was all he said.

It's true, my dad was a tough bloke and he'd lived a tough life like most of his generation, but my brother was no softie – not even slightly. After six years he left the air force and went straight to work in an electrical business in accordance with his trade qualifications. He was soon the boss of that business and soon after that he started his own business and did very well.

He's not very big my brother but he's stocky and tough. He used to collect his own debts – if you owed him money, he'd pay you a visit at your home. I remember him teaching me how to fight with a knife when I was thirteen – you'd have been very unwise to be on the wrong side of my 'big' brother.

I don't know if Dad's generation was tougher than my brother's, though I expect they were, but what I'm sure of is this, my dad came home a decorated hero from a war we won that everyone supported; my brother came home from a war we lost that many were against. There's a big difference between the two.

My sister Carolyn was an amazing young lady who in some respects lived in a time where there was less expectation and I imagine things seemed simpler. People worked hard and there weren't all the advantages provided by the technology we have, but your life and future seemed more readily defined. You went to school, got a job, got married and had children. That's a simplified version, but in a nutshell, that was what people expected would happen. I wonder how many women today, who can't find Mr Will Do let alone Mr Right, would love the simplicity of my sister's time.

Carolyn was beautiful, intelligent, vivacious, outgoing and popular. She'd been the captain of her school and was much loved and respected. She did well in high school but didn't have aspirations for further education. She flatted with girlfriends, travelled, and settled into a job as a secretary. It was a time in history where there wasn't a lot of expectation as to what a daughter would do. That's how it was – happiness was considered to be brought about by marriage, children and being a full-time mum, at least until all your children were in school.

Carolyn married at twenty-three and had two children by twenty-six, Darren and Danielle. But after the birth of her second child, there was something wrong. Carolyn had Hodgkin's disease.

If you got Hodgkin's disease at that time, it killed you – it was just a matter of how long you could last. Carolyn was in the final stage when diagnosed so her prognosis wasn't at all positive or hopeful. She was a fighter and had two little kids – she wasn't going to be taken from them, but she was. Carolyn was not quite thirty-three when she died. She'd battled for seven years – no-one had lasted that long before her.

I'd just turned nineteen and was oblivious to everything around me, utterly self-absorbed and interested only in pursuits that culminated in the conquest of females. I was a piece of work, that's for sure. I knew Carolyn was sick, but it's as if I wasn't paying any attention. My mum and dad came home from the hospital and I was lying shirtless on the lounge watching TV. Mum said to me, 'Carolyn died tonight.' I have tears in my eyes – I had them before I finished typing my mother's simple, three-word sentence. That's because I know what a useless, uncaring sack of shit I was.

Stunned, I looked at my mum and said, 'You're kidding.' Imagine that; of course my mother wouldn't walk into the room and joke about the condition of my poor dying sister.

It's one of the many things I'll never forgive myself for. I knew Carolyn was sick, but hey, it never occurred to me she'd die – how could she possibly die? People don't die? Do they? What a fuckwit I was.

Carolyn's funeral rammed home for me just how loved she was. The church was packed to overflowing – hundreds and hundreds of people. I met a couple of blokes who'd gone to school with her and hadn't seen her in nearly twenty years.

It is said that for a parent, the worst possible thing that can happen is for your child to predecease you, and that was the case for my mum. It crushed her. She carried Carolyn's loss with her forever.

My sister's poor distraught husband, Paul, had a responsible executive position and it must have been very hard to find himself a widower at thirty-seven and with two small children to raise. My parents, mum in particular, stepped into the breach and for the next several years, essentially raised my niece and nephew. It's a blur to me what I was doing, though I expect I wasn't any help.

As is evident, despite having two sisters and a brother, I was really more like an only child because the age gap between us was such that they were gone from the family home by the time there was any chance I'd notice them. It convinced me I didn't want to have a child who would be without siblings. I'm very much of the opinion that I'd have been a more rounded and better person earlier in life if I hadn't been on my own.

My dad was in a job with a great deal of responsibility. In my early life he was general sales manager for Samuel Taylor Pty Ltd, which was then a privately owned entity and the producer of Pressure Pak products. These included Mortein fly spray, Aerogard insect repellent, Gossamer hairspray, Santa Snow for Christmas decorations, Fabulon for ironing, Preen pre-wash spray, to name a few, as well as Y-Cough for colds and Trix detergent.

It was a big job. As a private entity, the structure was such that the only people senior to dad were the owner and his son. Before I was a teenager the company had been acquired by the international group, Reckitt and Colman, and Dad became sales director, and soon after, managing director and CEO.

It was a long way to come. Having left school at fourteen, my dad was now the CEO of one of Australia's most profitable and successful companies. Especially interesting given when he applied for a sales job at Samuel Taylor in 1947, they weren't hiring! He only got the job by offering to work two weeks for free so as to prove himself.

Bill Oldfield could only ever be called a 'man's man' – and how!

The Bill Oldfield I knew had a number of personalities. One of them being mischievous and my God he loved a bit of mischief. He had a wonderful sense of humour and the two combined made for pretty good company.

I loved being with Bill, having lunch, just sitting around and talking, and doing commercials with him, believe me, was an experience like no other.

Bill was a thoroughly good man.

– John Laws,
TV personality and legend of Australian radio broadcasting,
May 2018

I didn't see a lot of Dad when I was very young, but I don't feel deprived at all – I think he spent as much time with me as he reasonably could. He'd take me to Rugby on Saturdays and I remember getting up really early sometimes before school and we'd go for a swim in the ocean pool at Fairlight and then down into Manly for a loganberry pie with cream from The Manly Pie Shop. They'd just been baked an hour before and were still hot. I can see them now, and almost taste them.

I love that memory so very much, Dad waking me up and getting me out of bed with me still sleepy, but keen to go. On many days when I wake my own boys I visualise my dad waking me. My dad was a person who sprung out of bed. He understood responsibility, and nothing slowed him down. I'm like that now, at least in regard to my own sons. If it's about them, it doesn't matter how I feel, I just do it.

Probably as far back as I can remember, we always had a boat and Dad was mad for fishing, had been his whole life. It started really small, an 11-foot Quintrex – an open aluminium boat with an outboard. We went across the heads in that once, going from the spit to Manly. It was a little boat and it seemed like we were in the middle of the ocean. Next, Dad moved up to a 16½-foot plywood half-cabin cruiser. This was quite a leap. It had a small, V-shaped bunk section and Dad and I once slept on it while it was moored where he kept it at the marina in Fairlight. I can still hear the damn water slapping against the sides of the boat. I think I was awake all night – no doubt from excitement.

By the time I was in my mid-teens, the family boat had morphed into a company boat, which became a 24-foot Sea Ray, then a 32-foot Cresta and finally, a 49-foot Alaskan with a full-time captain. Samuel Taylor was the only division in the entire Reckitts worldwide group with its own boat. Late in the war, Dad had been in charge of procurements for the air vice-marshal of the air force – Dad had a reputation for being able to make things happen.

All in all, my dad wanted to spend time with me, and he did. He even took me interstate on a couple of business trips when I was eight and nine, and when I started high school, I would get a lift each morning with him, so we'd chat in the car, just like I do now every morning with my little boys.

In the 1960s, a lot of entertainment was brought about by a variety of guests and activities at home. My parents loved throwing a party and I was very much in my element serving drinks and hors d'oeuvres. In those days, the men mostly just drank beer and scotch and the ladies, were typically drinking moselle and riesling with perhaps someone occasionally opting for a shandy (beer and lemonade). My Auntie Lydia had a taste for those.

There would be the card nights, where several couples would turn up to our home to play canasta – does anyone play canasta today? A lot of interesting people popped into Mum and Dad's place – well I thought so.

One Saturday, when I was just a toddler, a very young man named Kerry Packer knocked on the door of our modest home in North Balgowlah. He was accompanied by Bill Buchanan, an executive working for Kerry's dad, Sir Frank.

It's a quirky story. Kerry had just gotten a new car and wanted to show it off, so he and Bill were driving around Sydney visiting. Kerry, at that stage, wasn't the heir apparent – his brother Clyde was in line to take over at that time. Amongst the things Bill Buchanan did for Sir Frank was keeping an eye on young Kerry. Imagine my poor mother as she answered the unexpected knock on the door, her hair in a scarf and midway through vacuuming the house.

For all Dad's toughness, there was one mistake I think he made with me – he wasn't tough on me. He didn't drive me and push me and I'm sorry he didn't do that. I needed to be pushed; I needed to learn discipline and to be responsible in every sense and he should have been harder on me. I can only guess why neither he nor Mum were tough on me. I think it was because so much of their lives had been difficult and hard. Maybe it caused them to be too gentle with me – I'm just guessing.

And when I note the hard nature of their lives, it was the early part of their lives. Once the simple matters of the Great Depression and the horrors and losses of WW II were behind them, things were looking good. Maybe it was also that it was a new era. It was the sixties and if you'd been born around World War I, there would have been a lot of things, especially socially related to young people that must have been hard to accept.

Then came the seventies, perhaps an even stranger decade? I was allowed to grow my hair long. My parents resisted at first, but by the time I was fourteen, it was touching my shoulders.

It's true I was rebellious and had my own ideas about things, and I don't mean just having long hair. My mother said I was 'uncontrollable', but while I might have seemed that way to Mum and Dad, I clearly had quite a bit of personal control because despite all the insane, dangerous and downright foolish things I did, I always very consciously steered clear of drugs. In my youth, I was surrounded by drugs – I was the only kid I knew who didn't at least smoke marijuana. Not much has changed; even at certain parties these days, it isn't uncommon for me to be the only person not snorting cocaine or dropping something.

I think my parents did a great job. They loved me as parents should love their children and either or both would have taken a bullet for me. I couldn't have asked for more and I'm thankful on a daily basis that I was their son. I wish they'd imparted to me more of the discipline and organisational abilities they exuded themselves. But now while I'm writing, I realise they must have done that because when I want to be, I'm disciplined and organised beyond belief. I suppose the key is 'when

I want to be', and I've demonstrated that throughout my life, but perhaps not seen it as clearly before – I couldn't have done the things I've done, or succeeded as I have, without discipline and organisation.

That shows I'm still learning about my parents and still learning about myself. Life is so crazy and strange and screwed up in so many ways, but you know that, right? Such is the downside of being human, and, in my case, an over-thinker.

The lessons they taught me finally sank in. It took a while, and even though they're gone, their lessons are still guiding me. I say things to my children that my parents said to me and I hear Mum and Dad saying those things to me whenever I say them to my boys.

My mum loved me and worked for me as long as she could. I can see her in her seventies wearing running shoes and out and about putting flyers in letterboxes or dressed to the nines and standing at a polling booth giving out how-to-votes. I didn't deserve her, though she wouldn't see it that way.

It would be hard for young people today to understand my mother's early life, or that of the children of her generation. She was born June Emma Hawkins on 17 November 1923. As an eight-year-old, my mum had a burst appendicitis and developed peritonitis. She was in a ward with nine other children and she was the only one who survived. How she survived, I don't know. There weren't any antibiotics, so if you got peritonitis, you died, just like the other nine kids in her ward.

Mum told me how the surgeon who operated on her came to visit her and said, 'Here's the little girl I took apart and put back together again.' The scars she had from that made her look like she'd been cut in half, but he saved her.

They say what doesn't kill you makes you stronger, and while for many things that would be rubbish, sometimes it would be true. I'd reckon a child surviving peritonitis while all those around you were dying and being quietly carried away would toughen you.

Mum also beat oesophageal cancer, which is nearly impossible. Generally, most people are dead within a couple of years, but mum was thirteen years beyond it when she died, and it wasn't the cause of her death. She was diagnosed at seventy-eight, which was beyond the age they'd operate, but I convinced the surgeon to make an exception. I've been quite convincing at times.

My mum was slight, though reasonably robust. I think she was more mentally strong than physically. She seemed to cope with a lot of things that went wrong. She just made herself like that – discipline.

She was a Scorpio and loved reading the stars. For years, she'd cut mine out of the newspaper whenever she thought there was something good and give them to me when I popped in to visit her. I'm a Cancer. Scorpios and Cancers are said to get along very well and neither my mum nor I were serious believers in the stars, but I think she liked whatever was positive that she thought might somehow be helpful to me.

When my mother put her violent first husband out the door she needed to support her two children without financial assistance from him – she chose that to avoid him having contact. She did the unthinkable for the late 1940s; she went to a bank and convinced them to lend her 500 pounds. That was about one and a half years pay in those days and the money was to start a business – risky, without security, and lending a woman (a single one at that) money was virtually unheard of then.

My mother could sew and that's what she used the 500 pounds for. She set up a business designing and making clothes – frocks, fancy petticoats, hooped skirts and wedding dresses. She was quite the designer and I still have some of her drawings. Soon, she was not only selling privately, but to department stores as well, and she had six other ladies sewing for her. All out of her flat in Bondi and other homes – the original sweatshops!

There was my mum, a female entrepreneur and ahead of her time. Living with her was her own mum, my grandmother, Violet. Mum was doing well for her family at a time when women really didn't have much of a place in business.

In the seventies she revived her design career for a bit of fun and designed a line of fashionable upmarket ladies raincoats. Mum also got the travel bug when I finished school and made an enjoyable career of organising large groups for international holidays. On a couple of occasions, the groups she coordinated were so large they chartered jumbo jets.

My mother wasn't a feminist in any way and I'm sure she'd find much of the notion of feminism quite silly. She was a smart, strong woman who succeeded against the odds from the beginning. She was ahead of her time, but lived appropriately and responsibly in her time. She never felt downtrodden or discriminated against by virtue of being born female.

June Oldfield was what she wanted to be: mother, wife, lady, businesswoman. She was all of those things by intent and design, without ever entertaining the idea she somehow played roles that were constructed by a male-dominated society.

Towards her end, my mum probably could have gone on for a few more years. She had a level of dementia but otherwise she seemed to still be reasonably okay. But then, as is so often the case, she had a fall and broke her hip. They mended her hip, but rehabilitating her wasn't successful. I don't think she had the will to live any longer and so she declined quite rapidly. When I would see her, she would be in and out of consciousness. Sometimes I would just sit with her and hold her hand; if she awoke, she was always glad I was there.

One day when she was drifting in and out, I told her my dad and her mum and her grandpa were all waiting for her and I said Carolyn (my sister) was waiting too, and it's been a long time since Carolyn has seen you. I said, we all love you so very much, but you go when you want to mum, it's Carolyn's turn to be with you again. Mum died the next day. I like to think she went because I said it was okay.

For the last few years of her life, I used to pray she would at least get to ninety because in my own mad thoughts I believed if I had that time, I'd be able to do more for her. By coincidence, or maybe divine intervention, she got those last few years and she made it to three weeks past her ninetieth birthday. Up until the last days of her life, I'd have put her in intensive care and had her plugged into anything to keep her alive, but all of a sudden, I realised I was doing that for me, not for her.

I miss my dad terribly. He died in his ninetieth year in 2008 and I don't think a day goes by that I don't think of him. I had to stop here for a few minutes to collect myself – I can't think of my dad without crying. If only I could hug him. I sometimes see him in my dreams and even cry then – sometimes I wake up with my face wet with tears.

Perhaps you think that pathetic, not the stuff of a grown man, but I don't mind, it's the truth – I love my dad. I'm sorry he was gone before my sons could know him, and he them, and I'm sorry I wasn't a better son, but whatever his reasons, I know he was enormously proud of me – more so than I deserved.

My dad's death was unexpected; I'd been told by the doctor he would go on for many months. Lisa and I were going away for the weekend and I'd checked with the hospital that very day to be sure Dad's condition was stable. We were almost out of mobile range when the call came through. I saw the number and knew immediately it was the hospital. Contrary to what I'd been told only a few hours before, I now get the frightful news my dad was going very quickly and may not last an hour. Up until that time, it was certainly the worst moment of my life – we were at least ninety minutes away. We did a U-turn and headed back as quickly as possible.

If you haven't had the experience, it will be hard to imagine what it's like to be far enough away that you know it's likely you can't make it in time. It's impossible to adequately describe the pain I felt – my dad was about to die and I probably wasn't going to get to him to say goodbye. It was one of those times when things are beyond anything you can do yourself and so you call upon unearthly powers to somehow help you – one of those times when the atheists manifest beliefs.

As it turned out, whether it was by design or plain luck, my dad held on and I spent about six hours with him. There wasn't much I could say and there was nothing I could do and the pragmatic doctor telling me he would die that night served no purpose at all.

I was a complete mess. Neither before nor since have I felt so helpless in every respect. I wasn't praying for him to somehow pull through because it didn't occur to me that was at all possible. They were giving him lots of morphine, and now I of course know they were assisting his death.

My mum was there and Lisa and a few other relatives, but at the end, it was just Dad and me. I was so sad, so powerless, so guilty for not being a better son.

I kept saying, 'I love you Dad.' I told him he was the best dad in the world and that one day I would have sons and I would tell them all about him and that they would love him too. Then I told him he was going to die. Through all this, he'd been lying there on his back, his eyes closed, and the only movement was his breathing, but then a single tear ran down the outside of the corner of his right eye.

He slowly breathed out, and didn't breathe in again. I sat there holding his hand until they came to take him away. I don't know why I told him he was going to die. I still don't know; maybe one day I'll work that out.

My dad was the bravest man I'd ever known, and he'd demonstrated that his whole life – there must have been times he was scared, because you can't be brave without first being scared. If there is no fear, there is no bravery – it's overcoming fear that is true bravery. He is my hero.

My dad's funeral was well attended by his many post WW II friends and those who didn't know him as such, but respected him, especially so from the local Returned Serviceman's League. There were former work colleagues, including those who saw him as a mentor, and a lot of people who didn't have to be there, but had taken the time to honour my dad and to bring us comfort.

I considered the words I would say at Dad's funeral would be the most important I'd ever written, but I was so close to falling apart and couldn't show it. A lot of people make the mistake of thinking I'm cold – if anything, I'm too emotional, but for the most part, I keep it to myself.

Alan Jones did a piece for Dad on his show on 2GB – another example of the extraordinary decency for which Alan is often not credited.

> You will therefore be saddened as I was to learn of the unexpected passing of David Oldfield's father on Friday night.
>
> I understand David was with him at the end, and David's mother and family are traumatised by the passing. He was the CEO of Samuel Taylor, but that was perhaps the least significant aspect of his life.

David Oldfield's dad was a decorated combat veteran, commissioned from the ranks and a survivor of the hell of being a prisoner of the Japanese. He was one of the last of a generation of Australians of whom we most probably will not see the like.

– Alan Jones AO,
arguably Australia's most successful broadcaster.
Excerpt from on-air tribute to my dad on 2GB,
25 February 2008

When I was growing up, my dad was reasonably well known and everywhere we went, I was referred to as 'Bill Oldfield's son', but as time moved on and I became publicly known, people at large referred to him as 'David Oldfield's dad/father'. These days people often note my boys as 'David Oldfield's sons', but I'll be more than happy if the time comes where I am simply referred to as 'Harry and Bert Oldfield's dad'. Perhaps that is something of the circle of life?

I often think about the fact we will all one day be gone, as indeed will all those who knew us and all those likely to remember us – we will all be lost forever like almost everyone before us. It will be as if we had never existed. As long as the human race exists in its current organised form, there will be historical figures with lives documented for all time, but the rest of us will disappear as the loved ones we left behind follow us into the abyss. Eventually, time will effectively erase our existence. Our complete lack of any consequence is a terrible thing to contemplate. At least, that's how it is for me.

My parents mean so very much to me and yet, not so long from now, everyone who knew them, loved them and respected them, will be gone. I hate that so much; I hate that so very much – they deserved more.

Early Interests and Using Up My Nine Lives

In terms of my early life, I expect it might seem I was lonely, living the life of an only child because of the age difference with my brother and sisters, but I don't remember ever being lonely. It is likely accurate, however, that I naturally became a bit of a loner. I was content in my own company – I still am. I enjoy conversation and good company, but I'm quite adapted to entertaining myself and that probably comes from my childhood.

I was happy watching TV or creating battlefields in the garden. Kids today have so much access we never had. There were three TV channels when I was little and eventually a fourth channel, but that was it. You made most of your entertainment.

I was utterly fixated by war and all things related to it. I don't know why. Dad never talked about the war. He was silent on his own experiences and it was hard to get a word out of him about WW II until the 1980s. Perhaps it was just how kids were then – toy soldiers and building war-related models was a big deal. Then there was playing wars – toy guns and dressing up as soldiers was very common.

However, I may have taken it to a new level, perhaps because I spent so much time on my own and in that sense in my own world. I built extensive formal battlefields in a large section of the garden. It was serious stuff – I was cementing in little ponds to create swamps and beach landing areas to re-enact US Marine amphibious assaults. I would construct entire campaigns with hundreds of soldiers, dozens of vehicles and I'd even worked out how to create little explosions and smoke through the use of chemicals Dad really shouldn't have gotten for me.

Amongst this was my desire to absorb every facet and fact of warfare, especially relating to WW II. Before I was ten, I'd read Leon Uris's, *Battle Cry*, Norman Mailer's, *The Naked and the Dead* and Irwin Shaw's *The Young Lions.* I don't know if very many eight, nine and ten-year-olds were reading those sorts of books, but I lived them, especially, *Battle Cry,* though I was very disappointed by the film adaption. Then there was Audie Murphy, amongst the greatest individual soldiers in history: to have cheated death so many times and die in a light plane crash. I was greatly saddened by his death, but I'm still inspired by his life. I read a lot of books children generally wouldn't and I absorbed an enormous amount of history, as well as a vast array of knowledge of the function of countless weapons, primarily small arms.

All of this without any knowledge that my dad was a genuine decorated combat veteran and could have told me firsthand about war in ways I could never get from a book. Ultimately, I got a lot of Dad's stories, but not from him, from others and from books and newspaper clippings and from finding out what his medals were for. I have no recollection whatsoever of my dad ever mentioning the war until I prised it out of him when I was an adult.

It was 1994 before I could get Dad to attend an Anzac Day march. It has been put to me that the blokes who were really amongst it were the ones who never talked about it and Dad certainly fitted that.

Unofficially, I had my first gun when I was eight years old. It was an eleven-shot pump-action Browning .22 repeater and I really shouldn't have had that gun, but in the 1960s, guns weren't thought of as they are today. I used to shoot in my backyard in suburban Balgowlah. Guns were just kept under a bed or in a closet and ammunition was generally stored with the gun.

When I was in the army cadets in high school, we had over one hundred .303 rifles and four Bren light machine guns in store at the school. The only thing standing between the crims and all those guns was a padlock. Like I said, different times – today, they'd be gone on the first night. Apart from the .22, I also had a slug gun (air-pump operated) and the kids in my street used to have slug gun wars where we would shoot at each other. I know – it's crazy! I think it's crazy! These slugs really hurt if you got hit and there is no doubt you'd likely blind someone if you hit them in the eye, but we were really careful and only ever aimed for body shots. Yes, not taking headshots was our idea of being careful.

The only time anyone got hurt was when I was defending the Robinsons' apartment up the Jackson Street laneway and Richard (my neighbour) led an assault up the lane. I hit him in the throat, but it was his fault – at the last second, he leapt into the air! Always safety first, in this case I was firing over Richard's head. Why he jumped up I'll never know. Gee he was angry. And bleeding!

The only time the police got involved was when I tried my new rocket formula with a launch from North Harbour Reserve in leafy Balgowlah Heights. I was eleven at the time, and quite the chemist! The resultant explosion smashed windows in Fairlight (adjoining suburb), and to this day, police are still doorknocking local homes looking for a kid called 'Oldy'. I know you're tempted, but don't phone 000 and tell them it was me.

My attempts at making rocket fuel caused me to happen upon an explosive formula and I put that to good use in our tunnelling days. Perhaps we were influenced by the Vietcong – I don't remember, but some friends and I got the idea to dig a series of tunnels as a secret HQ in the bush area of our local creek, and the mini-bombs I made were just the ticket to shift lots of dirt. In the interests of safety, I won't describe how I made those pocket explosives, though I suspect the internet could likely tell anyone interested how to do something similar – gee the internet is dangerous!

It's a miracle I survived my childhood and no-one else got seriously hurt. The rock wars, slug-gun fights, bomb making and expeditions to really dangerous places are testament to how bloody lucky we were. I'm sure other kids of our generation didn't fare so well.

The positive side to all this is that as a dad now myself, I know all the tricks – I know what they might do. I'm particularly worried about Bert in this regard, but unlike me with my dear dad, Bert will never be able to convince me to buy specialised industrial strength chemicals for his 'experiments'.

Included in Dad's various specialties during the war, he was also in charge of small-arms instruction for aircrews. Dad didn't have a gun himself – he didn't like guns very much, which makes me wonder why I was allowed to have them. His own distaste for firearms didn't stop him from teaching me the finer points of gunnery; he had, after all, been a gunnery officer and instructor and also taught combat pistol shooting.

Not long after I got my first gun, we went hunting. Dad was going to teach me that too, even though he wouldn't kill anything himself. It probably seems odd to teach your son something you wouldn't do, and for that matter to actually excel at something you won't do, but that was my dad. Maybe he thought I might need those skills one day, I don't know. I was nine at the time, so I'm just guessing again. From what I've read, a lot of people who've killed in war don't particularly want to shoot or kill anything again. I think Dad was like that.

I know he brought an American .45 ACP (pistol) home from the war, but soon after disposed of it. He told me many years later he didn't like it being in the house. Later in life, I'd own one of those myself. I know from others that he killed the enemy. I know there were times he was close enough to see their faces. Yet late in his life, when I asked him if he'd shot down any Zeros (fighter aircraft), all he said was, 'shared in a few'. He wouldn't tell me what I already knew.

I became quite proficient at hunting. I got to be quite adept at quietly getting in very close – careful, I might sneak up on you. And over time I became competent in the use of a variety of small arms, pistols included.

I once amazed people by shooting a running feral animal from the hip, in the dark, off the back of a moving vehicle. Luck? Probably. To the surprise of others, on another occasion, I headshot two very small feral animals, also in the dark at over 200 metres in tall grass – I expect that was luck as well. The two-ferals-in-the-dark incident occurred in the early days of One Nation – gee, didn't that start some rumours about who'd taught me to shoot.

I've been fortunate to shoot with the military and I got some great training thanks to American police instructors, but my dad was my first teacher. When he was quite old, and well after his seventh hip replacement, I bought Dad a .357 magnum revolver and we'd have father and son evenings at the range.

I'm kind of rusty these days; the times of reloading my own ammunition and firing over 500 rounds a week in practice are long gone. I still hit what I'm aiming at, just not necessarily exactly the spot I'm aiming at.

For the record, I haven't killed anything in more than fifteen years and I don't expect to ever shoot at an animal again. I don't judge others who hunt, but I'm sorry I ever did and I don't want my sons to ever kill. I spend a lot of time these days trying to make it up to animals and teaching my boys never to hurt any creature they don't absolutely have to.

I had pet dogs as a child, Ginger and Kimmy. I lost Ginger after his first birthday – he was an Australian terrier and a roamer who was hit by a car. I was devastated. Kimmy lived a full life – she was a beautiful girl.

However, I was without pets from fourteen until Lisa and I moved in together, when she bought a cockatiel for me that I named Audie. It was love at first sight. I took Audie everywhere. She used to sit on my computer screen at work and she'd sit on my shoulder when out and about. I even took Audie to parties and she'd hop in the shower with me and afterwards I'd blow-dry her as she'd lift up her little wings. She was such a smart girl and we were bonded beyond belief – her death crushed me. Is it weird that I have her preserved and plan on her being buried with me? Probably.

Audie was the turning point for me with animals. Her bond with me impacted me to such a degree that I came around to the thinking that all animals are precious and in need of our protection – from other humans of course. I will always be sorry it took me so long to come around to that thinking. I'm ashamed of what I used to do and will continue to do whatever I can for animals.

Now I have Alby the cockatiel. He isn't as bonded as Audie was, but I'm the only person he'll come to – he bites everyone else. He sits on my shoulder while I work and often hangs out with me watching TV. He's nearly fifteen and I've had him since he was eight weeks old.

It goes well beyond Alby: there are also Lulu and Dinky, our Jack Russells, aged eleven and twelve – we've had them since they were puppies. Then there are the horses, Timothy, Tango, Kahlua and Tyrion. I love them all so much – I spend as much time as I can with each of them.

As I write this my beautiful girl Lulu is sitting at my feet. She's just been diagnosed with cancer and it's a hard time. We're considering treatment options and I'm giving her some of the special natural things I take – I'll do all I can for her. We also have snakes and an axolotl, though they're more for Lisa and the kids, but I help look after them as well – amazing how trusting and comfortable a snake can become.

Our house is something of a menagerie given all our animal companions and the wild cockatoos I feed most days. I'd have more animals, but the thing that stops me is it gets to being unfair – there is only so much of me to go around and I'm already spread thin in terms of giving them my attention.

David Oldfield could have been Harry Butler, Steve Irwin and Sir David Attenborough rolled into one. David's unstinting love of animals is another of his many fascinating dimensions.

Invariably at the table – wine flowing like the Murrumbidgee in full flood, a robust conversation swerving every which way – talk turns to animals, be it his love of horses or reptiles, the outrageous horror of the Japanese whaling industry or the plight of animal victims of those barbaric live trade exports. His hate of animal cruelty makes his eyes glow with anger.

To visit the Oldfields' is like revisiting *Green Acres* – in place of Arnold the pig watching TV, there's Tyrion the miniature horse trotting through the house, or Shelley the carpet python slithering elegantly under the coffee table, or assorted water dragons languishing by the pool. For David, it's nirvana, and I'm not talking about the rock band.

– Craig Bennett,
entertainment reporter, confidant to the stars and snake wrangler,
February 2018

My love of the military meant that at one stage I expected I would become a soldier. Yes, it would have been the army for me, though when my parents nearly relocated to the USA, I thought I'd be a marine. God, how different it would have been: I was almost an American! One thing led to another and going into the military didn't happen. If Australia had been at war when I was the right age, I would have gone; I would have felt it my duty. I would have been compelled to follow in the footsteps of my father, brother, uncles, great uncles and so on. I suspect a lot of people wouldn't understand that.

I'm extraordinarily lucky that never happened. When you're a boy, you don't see the ugliness and the death, the heartache and the loss, the terror and the pain. From what I can see, war is all those things and nothing good. Lucky I didn't go is an understatement.

My love of westerns and war movies and anything relating to history and dates, moments in time that were of great consequence, people, personalities, the human condition, have filled my head with what many might consider trivia, but it's only trivia if it's not important to you.

I was one of those kids who was pretty much able to do whatever I tried. Clearly I was better at some things than others, but I was competent at anything I put my mind to. These days, it's perhaps a case of 'can't teach an old dog new tricks', he says as he reaches for a pen and paper instead of using the calculator on his iPhone!

There was a tenpin bowling centre only a few hundred metres from where I lived, so it wasn't long before I started bowling. Contrary to some beliefs, bowling is an active sport that exercises and strengthens various parts of the body. If you're doing it once a fortnight, you're probably not getting a lot out of it, but if you're bowling thirty to forty games a week, as I did, you're getting a lot of exercise. It also requires considerable concentration and a good eye.

I got good enough to win lots of regional and state competitions in singles, doubles, teams, all events and Masters, and when I was sixteen, a young lady and I were Australian Junior Mixed Doubles Champions in the same year four associates and I won the Australian Open Teams Championships.

Perhaps inevitably, I did some work in the bowling industry. I repaired machines, and it was there that I had one of my close shaves with death. I was working on an electric motor. A silly mistake caused me to get an electric shock. I was frozen in place with 240 volts pouring through my body. You'd probably need to experience this to truly understand the effect, though I don't recommend that. I was held in place – I couldn't move – I was in essence melting where my hands were in contact with the cables and the rest of me was just stuck. There was no getting away. I completed the circuit from active to earth, which sent electrical current straight through my heart. It's the worst way to get zapped – you die in a matter of seconds! There was a very specific feeling; it was as if my body was a box and my heart was on its own in the middle fighting to keep going. An electrician friend said it would have been as if my heart was in a vice, and that's about right.

As is the stuff of timing and miracles, a co-worker who shouldn't have been around, decided to pop out of the workshop to see how long I'd be, and he turned off the power. It seemed like several seconds passed as the current slowly receded from my body. I felt kind of limp. I climbed out of the machine and burst out laughing while slapping this fellow on the back and explaining he'd saved my life. He had no idea what had happened. He thought I had my hand caught in the machine.

Skin in places on my fingers and hands was blackened and had melted like plastic, but there was no pain. I sat in the workshop eating my dinner and my legs started to involuntarily twitch and jump. At that point I rang the front desk and suggested they call an ambulance. After many tests and much examination, the doctors at St Vincent's Hospital informed me I only survived because I had an unusually strong heart, which'll seem odd to those who claim I don't have a heart. Not quite seventeen, I went through some very painful skin grafts to repair my fingers and hands. To this day, I have the strangest of heartbeats!

If almost being killed by electric shock wasn't enough, a year later I was nearly burned to death. How I lived to twenty is a case in point! I was the passenger in the two-seat van version of a little old Mini. This car had its battery sitting in a recessed area behind the driver's seat and there was a flammable aerosol can in the back that rolled down and wedged between the battery terminals. Don't ask me why the battery terminals were exposed or tell me how unlucky it was that the can was just the right size to get wedged between them. Heat, I suppose, melted the solder of the seam on the can and the next thing, pressurised liquid fire was spraying between the two fronts seats, and the car appeared to be engulfed in flames.

The car was on fire, I was on fire and the driver was on fire – what a sight that must have been, but with my luck still holding, we were stopped at traffic lights when it happened. Imagine if we'd been speeding along at the time? I released my seatbelt with my right hand, opened the door with my left hand, turned to look for cars coming up beside us (we were in the middle lane) and as it was clear, I then rolled across the road to put myself out and stood up just off the road.

I was still smouldering, but I looked back in horror to see the driver was still in the car unable to release his seatbelt. I ran to the car and as I opened the driver's door, he finally got the seatbelt undone and leapt from the car. We retreated from the road and looked back to see that the fire appeared to have gone out. Apparently, once the aerosol can was empty, the flames receded.

A later investigation showed the fire had been lapping at the exposed plastic fuel line and a few more seconds of flame and the fuel would have ignited – my chum would have been toast, and me too if it happened as I ran to his aid.

I had 20 per cent of my body burned – right arm and torso mostly – and fortunately it was predominately superficial and first degree, but gee it hurt! I spent eight days in hospital. Oh, and my favourite tie, along with a nice shirt and pair of pants, were completely destroyed. Chalk that one up to experience and beware of young people driving old cars!

If you haven't already noticed, I'm apparently quite casual about deadly things happening to me. I'm not sure why I'm like that, but it's a good thing. I'm cool-headed in a crisis, and I would come to demonstrate that in many dangerous incidents throughout my life.

The fellow who burned with me in his little Mini van was a guitar player named Peter O'Mara. He's relatively well known in jazz circles and has a professorship of jazz guitar at the Munich conservatorium of music, but back in the day, he and I were in a band together. Yes, I'd gotten the 'rock star' bug and so I joined a bunch of guys around my age and we had a lot of fun playing little venues. I was the lead singer.

All these guys were vastly more talented than me. O'Mara in particular was such a natural – he could play anything, construct harmonies and I think he was an all-round musical genius, but he found rock too simple, moved on to jazz and has done enormously well in that genre.

I formed another group, got a little better and started touring here and there and even when not far from home, generally played three to four nights a week for audiences of anywhere between 200 and 1500. We had three roadies, a bus and some very good equipment. These were amongst the best years of my early life and it led me to lots of opportunities teenage boys enjoyed.

I was still quite shy, but performing on stage must have cleared some of that for me and thinking back on the outfits we wore, it probably would have been difficult for anyone to grasp that the lead singer was kinda shy. I still have some of the leather pants, though no-one gets in them anymore, me included, and the matching velvet outfits were simply to die for! The hair, the flares, the big wide-collared silky shirts – I expect it's hard for a lot of people to see me like that. I have a lot of great memories from back then and one or two things I'm less than proud of, but hey, I was seventeen, eighteen and nineteen, and no-one should be surprised.

Do things go in cycles? Maybe. Bowling had taken me away from diving, but damaging my hands as I did with those burns took a toll on my bowling prowess, so I did my years in bands and then jumped into diving full-time. I've included a chapter on what diving taught me and some of the crazy, life-threatening situations I experienced beneath the waves.

Has danger always beckoned me? I really don't know, but I think I'm too adventurous and too much of a risk-taker. Even today, I'm still a little too adventurous, though I've scaled back a lot because of my sons. Having them makes me more conscious of the need to be careful with my own life. And after all, I'm still here, though I don't take lightly the amount of luck attached to that being the case and I fear for what my sons may get up to. I hope I can engender them with my capacity for survival, while also giving them enough common sense to be careful at all times.

In 1986, the National Diving Championships were to be held in Manly, where I lived, so I thought, oh well, close to home, I'll give it a go. My experience and qualifications led to me being made captain of the New South Wales scuba team, and as an individual I entered the open scuba and underwater photography competitions.

The open scuba was run in five parts, all done to speed against the clock. There was search and recovery, natural navigation, navigation with a compass, underwater obstacle course and a comprehensive theory test. I won and hence became the Australian Open Diving Champion.

There are lots of underwater photography competitions, but few if any are like the Australian Underwater Federation's testing. Usually, a photographer submits a variety of photographs, perhaps ten or twenty, and these are judged. The problem with this approach is a serious underwater photographer will take thousands of photos in a year. It's common to fire off thirty shots or more of one subject, in the pursuit of that single perfect photograph where lighting, focus angle and subject are 100 per cent in tune.

Taking 5000 or 10,000 photos in a year and selecting and submitting your best ten for evaluation is questionable in terms of testing your supposed skill. Still, it's worth noting, with the equipment and environment taken into consideration, underwater photography is much more difficult than taking pics on dry land. In this national competition I entered, you had a three-hour window to take twenty photographs, being four each in five designated categories, such as shots of divers, fish and so on.

Judging was undertaken by officials selecting the best pic of your four pics in each category with the result being determined through those five photos. Not only did the photographs have to be good, you had to seek out certain marine life to comply with the category requirements and it all had to be done with that one roll of film.

I won that as well, so that year I was also the National Underwater Photography Champion. I didn't compete again – I quit competition diving while I was ahead. I didn't feel I had anything further to prove, and besides, I was busy with my diving businesses.

In 1987, my diving business took a serious hit that would prove to be a clear contributing factor in what I learned about the mercenary nature of things and the lack of interest in truth, as opposed to 'how much money can we make'.

An executive of Neptune Wetsuits chartered our dive boat, as he had in the past, so it wasn't one of our scheduled dives, but a specific midweek charter for a small group, not arranged by us. The Neptune fellow was not only a professional in the industry, but qualified as a divemaster and a very experienced diver. We supplied the boat and our driver; none of the participants were regular customers of ours apart from the fellow who arranged the charter.

To cut a long story short, one of the participants, a diver visiting from interstate, drowned, in a classic manner that was entirely diver error, brought about by inadequate training and experience. Had the dive been one of our scheduled dives where we were in charge, neither the diver in question nor his buddy would have been allowed on this particular dive.

Relatives of the deceased were looking for a way to sue us along with the dive shop that had taught the deceased to dive. Sadly, they connected us by virtue of our collection of a fee, which in reality was a contribution to the charter fee and agreed to by the divemaster who chartered the boat and also went on the dive.

I suspect that in the mind of any fair person, it would be concluded we had no responsibility for what happened, but sometimes one may be caught up in technicalities, especially when there is money to be made through a willingness to exploit circumstances rather than attribute blame genuinely.

I found myself working my business with the expectation that, at any time, I would receive notification the business was being sued – it meant someone was going to try and take away all I'd built.

It put me under a cloud for more than five years where I didn't know if I was working for me or someone who'd ultimately take what was mine. It was most discouraging, and as things dragged on I lost interest in working for something that may be taken from me. To say I was angry is an understatement in the extreme. I seriously faced losing everything and yet those arguably responsible, weren't targeted at all.

It turned out the divemaster who'd chartered our boat was an undischarged bankrupt without a penny realistically to their name, so the sad fact was there was no sense in going after him. They weren't seeking answers or justice, they were after compensation.

After spending money initially on legal advice, it became apparent the business wasn't placed to hire the legal team required for a trial in the Supreme Court of another state, or our own state for that matter.

It was now 1993 and the decision was made that I would defend the company – madness I hear you say. Normally, I'd agree. After all, it is said, the lawyer who represents himself has a fool for a client. However, in this matter, there were few in Australia so qualified as me to address the matters of this case. Not only was I an expert in analysing the causes of diving mishaps/deaths, but I was intimately connected to all the facts of the case. In some respects, it was going to be easier for me to deal with this case, than perhaps it would have been to try and explain the issues to an eminent expert in law, who had no understanding of diving.

I'm not recommending you ever attempt what I did – get yourself a good lawyer. Mine was an unusual case. It had some unique elements and it had me understanding that if I didn't get the company out of trouble, I would lose all I'd been building for the previous ten years.

I had to reside in Melbourne for a few weeks and appear in court each day doing my best impression of a lawyer. I spent my nights pouring through the day's transcripts and preparing for the battle of each following day. There I was, a legal eagle in the Supreme Court for eleven days, up against a QC and a barrister with solicitors assisting them.

I probably seemed cocky, but it was more that I was angry, knowing myself to be entirely in the right, but the quintessential victim of a dirty situation – not the legal system, but the unfortunate way it was being used.

On the first day it had to be determined whether the trial would be heard by a jury or a judge sitting alone. The QC and the barrister for the other side tried to convince me a judge sitting alone was in my best interests. Mmmmm, the opposition giving me advice? Yeah, of course I'll take that – hardly. I figured the only chance I had was to appeal to the jury by discrediting the case against my company; I figured a jury would be more interested in reasonable facts and attributable blame than legal technicalities.

I explained to my very eminent legal opponents (no joke, they were among the best), that I'd go with a jury. The barrister looked at me and said, 'You do realise that if you make a mistake and the jury has to be dismissed, you'll be up for all the costs and we'll have to start again.'

I was debating evidence, cross-examining witnesses and successfully discrediting and neutralising their experts. It was an extraordinary experience few non-lawyers would ever get, and I reiterate, don't try it yourself.

In the end, I got the company out of it. I managed a costs contribution that pretty much squared things up and the presiding Judge, Justice John Coldrey said, 'Thank you Mr Oldfield. You have some very valuable experience. If you give up diving, you might consider another profession in law.' (Victorian Supreme Court transcript, September 1993)

It was a huge win and an even bigger relief. A loss would have cost me my business, my building and almost everything else I owned, but I was left disturbed by the whole experience – the more than six years from the incident to the end of the court case had taken a toll on me. Within a few months I had sold my business and moved on – the joys of my youth, of diving and teaching diving across the waters of the globe, had come to an end.

Lisa and Me

I've had a lot to say about my mum and dad and being a dad myself, and I've mentioned my wife Lisa, but not had a lot to say about her. For a long time Lisa and I have had a love/hate relationship – in the beginning, we loved each other and then we hated each other! Sometimes there has been loathing and a bit of detesting thrown into the terribly toxic bile that is our relationship. It hasn't all been that bad; I was just setting the scene for you because there's certainly been a lot of media coverage as to the ugly nature of our family arrangements. When we did, *I'm a Celebrity … Get Me Out of Here!* together in early 2018, they billed us as 'Australia's most dysfunctional couple'.

Not long ago, when we had a couple of TV execs over for lunch, one of them asked me what sort of show I'd like to do next and I said, 'Widower wants a wife.'

When Lisa was asked on *The Real Housewives of Sydney* if she'd given thought to divorce, she said, 'I've never really seen myself as a divorcee, more as a widow.'

As you can see there's a bit of tit for tat and we must have both at times envisioned the other dying. It's fair to say there have been times when we have not been each other's favourite person and we have made that evident, occasionally on camera. I have loved Lisa and I have disliked her intensely and sometimes both of those things at once, and I expect she would be able to say something similar.

Just prior to Christmas 2018, and hence just before this book was to be published, Lisa and I separated. Many people who've watched our relationship over the years would say it was a long time coming, while others who know us well didn't think we would ever separate. It wasn't something I wanted, but there came a point where being together with Lisa was no longer in the interests of our sons.

No, I haven't been having an affair and getting divorced wasn't in my plans, but I did need to break the cycle of dysfunction and give our sons the very best chance in life that I could.

It is hard to know where it goes from here as there are so many issues that need to be addressed, but it's all about our boys and as long as I can provide a loving, nurturing and functional environment for them then it will be more than worth the horror and heartache that is the breakdown of our family. What is often almost momentary selfishness has a lifelong impact on the innocents, so like all things, the matter of separating or divorce needs to be thought through to its logical conclusion. It never ends well for the kids, unless perhaps there is violence and other abuse present, but even then it still doesn't end well; it is still a form of compromise rather than a best outcome.

Does anybody have a really great relationship, and if so, for how long? Lisa and I were married for seventeen years,which is five years past the average length of a marriage that ends in divorce. Indeed, everyone we know who was married around the same time as us is already divorced and some of them were divorced five or ten years into their marriage. Some have separated and then reunited after a year or two.

I'm not sure men and women are meant to be together long term. When I was a little boy (about eight) and clearly my parents were having issues, my dad used to say, 'You've got to be a good boy son, or your mother will leave us.'

Dad shouldn't have said that to me; it was wrong, but I understand the frustration he must have been feeling and I'm not concerned about it. I knew at the time there was no way Mum would leave me – she'd take me if she was going, but I wouldn't have wanted to leave my dad, so no good in that for anyone.

My parents were together for more than forty years after that time in my childhood, so clearly they got past it all and from what I could see, they got on about as well as could be expected. My mum had the classic line, 'I still love your father, but I'm not in love with him anymore.' I once read being 'in love', as such only lasts at most for around three years. If so, marrying somebody you like, and with whom you have much in common, would be the sane approach. Ah, being sane and being in love – right here, now, is perhaps the first time you've seen those two things noted in the same sentence.

Children complicate a couple's relationship and I suspect my mum and dad stayed together in part because of me, but that was clearly just through a rough period from which they recovered, so they weren't meant to break up and me being there put it off till it was no longer seen as necessary.

Kids need their parents, both their parents, and they need them to be good parents, or at least for those parents to have an amicable arrangement/relationship. Anything less is a compromise, though many fool themselves into thinking otherwise. It comes back to the kids and what it is you are willing to lose for what you believe your life could otherwise be – anything else you're doing, you're doing for yourself, not the kids.

There is no doubt how hard we need to try to get along – relationships are hard as hell, sooner or later – if you've been in a marriage for ten years or more and not had those experiences, I suspect you may not know how unusual and lucky you are.

I love Lisa, but we're so different in so many ways – in almost every way. I'm logical, responsible, into food health, and often feel like I spend my days trying to live forever. Lisa eats whatever she wants and smokes and I have great difficulty understanding why she can't muster the willpower to give it away. We're almost opposites and yet it didn't seem at all like that in the beginning, perhaps because we weren't so different then. Yep, these days, it seems we have almost nothing in common, except our boys; but that, even on its own, is a lot to have in common.

Once upon a time Lisa and I enjoyed each other's company and she used to tell everyone I was her best friend. We loved each other's dark, macabre sense of humour, horseriding, bushwalking, shooting, snow skiing, movies, and history and events. It seems there was a time when we were much alike.

To finish on Lisa, I'll go to where it started, so out of the blue and unusual in itself. We met in a taxi. I was coming home from Broken Hill and Lisa was returning from Brisbane. It was 24 March 2000. It was a Friday night with easily 150 people at the taxi rank at Sydney Airport. I was already in the cab when the driver checked if I was okay with taking another person going the same way.

The cab driver hopped out and started yelling, 'Manly, anyone going to Manly?' I was in the front and noticed, in the side mirror, a pair of ankles step off the kerb and start walking towards the cab. I've always been a bit of an ankle man! This beautiful, tall young lady (twenty-five at the time) climbed into the seat behind me. I could see her in the rear-vision mirror; she was stunning; she looked liked a young Xena Warrior Princess with her hair cut as it was and her blue eyes, symmetrical face and high cheekbones.

I was generally attracted to blondes, but now and again I'd do charity work for a brunette – again, my dark sense of humour. Lisa really stood out – physically appealing is an understatement in the extreme.

When we were nearly in Manly, she reached between the front seats and put her hand on my wrist and said, 'I couldn't help notice who you are, and I just want to tell you my family and I are grateful for the work you've been doing for people disenfranchised by Country Labor.'

Being naturally shy, I'm a bit of a sucker for a gorgeous forward young lady. I turned and said, 'That's not what I was expecting from your demographic.' Typical of me in many respects, I responded in a completely truthful and logical way though still highlighted my genuine surprise.

Once out of the cab, we exchanged numbers and after a lot of odd, inconclusive communications, we had a date here and there.

I was always aware Lisa was mysterious and playing footsie, but I couldn't quite pin it down. Eventually I determined she was in a relationship and going through the process of ending it and indeed, I was correct. When we met, Lisa was unhappily engaged and due to be married, funnily enough, to another fellow named David. Ending that was all very messy, though I thought he took it as well as could be expected. Not sure I'd have been so collected, all things considered.

By July we were dating and overnighting a few nights a week and by October, we moved in together. By April 2001 we were engaged and married in October that same year. It moved pretty quickly from sharing a taxi ride to sharing a home and a life, but Lisa was very keen and when it seems to be right, no sense mucking around. Plus, I was forty-three and not getting any younger, so I popped the question!

One day, before we were engaged, when my parents and I were having lunch with Lisa's parents, her dad suddenly raised that he was concerned about the age difference and I said, 'I am too, I usually date much younger girls, but I'm making an exception for Lisa.'

Actually, I didn't say that, but it was close to that. I quite innocently said, 'Oh, I've been out with girls younger than Lisa.' A response that caused Lisa's dad to nearly choke while blurting out, 'You should be in jail!'

In fairness to myself, I didn't mean it how it sounded. To me it was just a statement of fact and my way of saying to Lisa's dad that it isn't unusual. And it wasn't. I looked younger than I was and looking at us as a couple in those days, the age difference didn't seem anywhere near what it really was.

Not long after we were married, Lisa asked me, 'Why did you choose me?' Always the romantic, I responded, 'I was just tired.'

Close to Christmas 2009, Mum was whisked away in an ambulance. She went into total shutdown – her blood was acidifying, and her organs were on the brink. She was unconscious, thought to have a twisted bowel, and the doctors were convinced she would never awaken and die within days. I was desperate not to lose her and I whispered in her ear that Lisa was pregnant and she had to stay alive to be with her new grandchild. Did she hear me? Did she understand? I believe somehow that message got through, because within hours she started to improve, and to the doctors' astonishment, she made a full recovery.

That episode had the strangest twist: I'd told her a lie. There was no suggestion Lisa was pregnant, but I was willing to do anything not to lose her. Dad had told me the only acceptable lie is one told to help somebody else, though I acknowledge it's also unsustainable. I told the lie for me, not her. I was selfish not wanting her to go; I wasn't ready.

However, the lie turned out to be the truth, for unbeknownst to us, Lisa actually was pregnant and slightly over eight months later, our first son Henry arrived. What had started as a lie to give Mum incentive to live had turned into a wonderful truth, and so she got to know Henry, and nearly two years later Albert arrived, and they both got to know her. I'm glad I lied to her and I'm sure my dad would've understood.

I've been mostly fortunate in terms of opportunities to do the sort of work I wanted to do. Some say that if you love your work, then it really isn't work at all. I wouldn't go that far, but I would certainly nominate talkback radio as being the 'work' I loved the most. I'm not finished with work – there are a few things I'm still planning, so be aware, this book will end, but I'm not yet quite done.

These last years have been strange, conflicting and in some respects confounding. I'm sure some of the things I've done publicly haven't appeared to make sense, but of course that would be because much of the background of where it's all coming from is largely unknown beyond me, and hence wouldn't be understood by anyone else. It's a tad annoying at times when people so wrongly come to conclusions as to why I've gone in a certain direction, when they have no informed basis on which to judge me in any respect.

For a while now, my family and animals have been my only reason of consequence to be alive. I have been without purpose beyond that, but even as I write that now, surely that is purpose enough. There will always be the unseen and the unplanned and events that can unavoidably overtake me, but I can see where my life goes from here and most of that is taken up by my responsibility to others.

Given what I've been through, I'm in remarkable shape physically, especially internally, and I work a lot on that because my little sons need me to be ahead of the curve for my age and I'm well and truly conquering that challenge by always seeing it as a challenge.

As I write this, I have primary custody of Henry and Albert and I'm hopeful that will remain the case. I have been their primary parent/carer since Albert was six months old, so they are used to being with Daddy.

I've never considered myself to be a natural at being a father – I've had to really work at it. It's been a struggle for years now as I've been the glue that kept our family together, but the experience has made me a better dad and a better man than I otherwise would have been.

It is said, 'Necessity is the mother of invention' and I know that's true in my case. I have become what I have needed to become, and I continue to learn from the challenges I've endured.

What happens to me from here isn't important except in so much as what I need to do for my sons. I don't know how much fun lies ahead, but I do know I still have a lot to do and with a little luck and the guidance of my parents' voices in my head, there'll be quite a few smiles and more than my share of laughter yet to come.

My thoughts are pure, I've not been corrupted, and as foolish as even I know it seems, I believe in the necessity for good to mercilessly crush evil. I'm not sure I'll be here for that fight, but my boys likely will be, and I'll make sure they're ready.

Diving

I learned to dive, I taught others to dive and I owned multiple diving businesses. Those many years, starting from a very young age, have a lot to do with who I am.

It was through diving I had some of my earliest disappointments, with people and systems. Those experiences shaped me at an impressionable age, especially so in the matter of my views on human behaviour. I expect what I learned through diving gave rise to much of my cynicism, almost certainly my unwillingness to respect someone or something without it being earned, and it impressed upon me that plans must never rely on a single item – always have backup.

I didn't say what I experienced through diving caused me to learn about human behaviour – did you notice that? Do you see the difference? To learn something implies matters of fact, so I said those experiences shaped my views, because perhaps what I took in from the experience wasn't accurate. Maybe what I concluded from my observations was wrong. I always look very closely at being wrong – I expect that surprises a lot of people; or maybe I'm wrong?

There was a time, when I was quick to kill virtually anything at all – sadly, I must have derived some pleasure from it – an awful thought, but perhaps it isn't uncommon. I've seen it in many children, my own included – the ease with which they will go out of their way to step on an ant or burn a bug to death with a magnifying glass – there seems to be a certain level of natural cruelty in children, or is it mostly just boys?

I don't know the answer, but I know it's terribly wrong to kill even so much as an ant, just for the hell of it – perhaps it's something most people grow out of and perhaps the ones who don't, grow up to be very ugly dangerous people. That's a matter for the shrinks, and something that is likely very explainable, but unlikely to ever be changed. Some humans are going to grow up bad and society probably doesn't want the truth on how and why that happens.

These days I don't kill anything, but that is in stark contrast to the days I so very much regret, when I subscribed to the view, kill anything that moves – if it doesn't move, prod it and then kill it. Even now, I make exceptions, I do kill mosquitoes, flies and cockroaches, but that's it – if a dangerous spider gets in the house, I catch it and let it go outside. In the case of funnel web spiders, I scoop them up and drop them off at my local vet to have their venom milked for antivenene. Recently, I relocated six red-back spiders that had taken up residence all around our front door. It was best for them and us that I found them somewhere else to live.

I'm absolute in teaching my sons not to ever kill anything you don't have to kill. There are things about me and things I've done that I don't want my sons to emulate.

For nearly twenty years I've been trying to make up for my awful crimes against other living creatures. It's a long way to come considering even my diving career started because I'd spearfished from the age of ten and only learned to scuba dive for the express purposes of getting down deeper to more easily spear and kill bigger fish.

Yet from the moment I became a scuba diver, I lost all interest in spearfishing. The underwater world was so fascinating to me that my wish for harmless adventure eclipsed that part of my personality focused on hunting and killing – at least as far as the ocean was concerned. I was enthralled by just being underwater. Even to this day, I love to swim underwater and I can find enjoyment and relaxation just lying on the bottom of a pool – no doubt some would find enjoyment in me staying there.

My youngest son, Albert (Bert) seems to have this in him too. He tries to spend most of his bath time with his head under the water, and at swimming lessons, his instructor spends all her time pulling him up off the bottom. Maybe the apple really doesn't fall far from the tree because my eldest son, Henry, shares Albert's love of underwater time as well.

Scuba diving today is so different to how it was when I learned to dive. Yes, I'm about to tell you it was tougher in my day – that's because it demonstrably was in every way.

In the first case, the equipment wasn't as good and much of the gear used today didn't exist when I started diving. The standout there is the BCD (buoyancy compensator device), sometimes BCV (vest as opposed to device). We didn't have them, which meant no floating on the surface. You had to tread water all the time and if you had any distance to swim on the surface, it really took a lot of effort.

Snorkelling any distance with scuba gear is difficult. The gear restricts movements and creates a lot of drag, and without anything to give you buoyancy, a person of average fitness gets tuckered out going 50 metres in a pool. It's much harder in the ocean. Under the water isn't as bad, but still difficult. Without a BCD, there is no way to compensate for wetsuit compression and so you were always heavy at depth. The deeper you went, the heavier you got.

Another reason it used to be harder to learn to dive is because there wasn't the 'continuing education' style of training that has now been common for forty years. When I started, there was little in the way of courses beyond the beginners' course that was generally referred to as basic scuba.

The beginners' course was pretty much all there was, so you had to learn much more in that one course, as it would be the only training you'd ever get. This often took the form of underwater commando training that very few people completed and my own experience at the very start puts it in perspective. The course I took as a fourteen-year-old ran for six weeks – about ten nights over the period and one full day of each of the six weekends. There was no pool training and the final exam was a full written test, not multiple choice. We were trained in things that these days are parts of advanced and specialised courses, yet we were only doing basic scuba. We were taught to be able to strip off all our gear on the bottom and make it to the surface, and how to swim out as a lifesaver to dive down and rescue a person off the bottom. We were expected to perform arduous tasks and do free-swimming ascents as part of out of air emergency training, and, like I said, it was a beginners' course!

I started with five other people. At the end of the course, I was the only person left, but not only that, I'd been the only person left since the start of week four – I was the only person still going from the halfway mark.

Most were just unable to keep up with the physical demands, something which was greatly lessened in later years by the introduction of BCDs. Divers today likely can't begin to imagine diving in a full wetsuit without a BCD. In the tropics, where little if any wetsuit is required, it's not as big an issue, though snorkelling on the surface wearing scuba gear still takes it out of you if you don't have a floatation device.

The idea of continuing diver education was just starting up in those early days, but a lot of the instructors weren't on board as such, so they were still teaching what amounted to survival courses.

As for the BCDs, the first models had virtually a life-vest appearance and the 'old timers', actually considered the vests were really for people who probably shouldn't be diving, as they were a crutch on which weak people could lean. Of course, that was the equivalent of caveman thinking. The BCD was an extraordinary invention and once you got used to them, you'd have been crazy to dive without one.

Apart from the assistance on the surface as a floatation device both for general use and in an emergency, the intention of the design was to have air added to them at any depth to compensate for wetsuit compression.

For those who are not aware, neoprene wetsuits, when cut open, look a bit like dark honeycomb or the old Aero chocolate. The material is filled with little gas pockets that are subject to compression as you go deeper under water. The amount of lead weight carried by divers is, however, generally determined by the weight needed to cancel out the buoyancy of the wetsuit on the surface. If you have the weight balance right, with all equipment in place, you should float on the surface, upright, at eye level, while holding your breath. As you exhale, you should start to sink. This is referred to as neutral buoyancy. It's a state were the diver is not really floating or sinking and overall buoyancy is determined only by the level of air in the lungs rather than any impact applied by equipment.

In this state, a diver may simply empty the air from their BCD, start to exhale and gently sink in an upright position. This is the most controlled way to descend (feet first) and also allows for the easiest method of equalising your ears as your lungs are lower than your head and the equalising process is assisted by air naturally rising into the airspaces including the middle ear. The BCD allows the diver to be truly balanced and, in effect, weightless – neither rising nor sinking, but rather, streamlined and able to move in the most optimal fashion underwater, while also providing surface buoyancy for resting or moving any distance on the surface.

This isn't a book on diving and I'm cognisant that all things considered, I'm going into quite a bit of detail here, but you see it is a book about why I am as I am; what I'm like and how that came about.

One of those things is that I can be something of a pedant! I hate things that are not explained – I hate that which is incomplete, and I hate being misunderstood or considered to have left something out. That's a lot of hate for lack of detail, but it's who I am, and in that, it's in keeping with the subject of this book to look at that aspect of my personality.

I cannot be so detailed on every individual matter throughout this book because it would be too long but diving in particular is a good place to look at why I'm like this because while diving is a marvellous adventure, it can go wrong in seconds, so it requires very precise thinking and preparation.

Much of what I learned about people at a relatively young age came about through my own mistakes in diving and seeing or looking in detail at the mistakes of others. Most people appear incapable of learning from the mistakes of others – it's like there is a wall between what others have got wrong and what we believe we can do ourselves. That crazy notion that 'it won't happen to me'. It's a nice thought, but invariably, humankind makes the same mistakes generation after generation, so it shouldn't be a surprise that as individuals we often make the same mistakes we've seen others make before us.

Diving is marketed as safe adventure, but the only reason huge numbers of people don't get killed diving is because of dumb human luck combined with what appears to be a level of survival instinct.

> At the anti-aircraft guns, the stern came into view. I felt relieved. At the stern, Mark's buddy was digging a hole in the sand and lowering his depth gauge into it. Mark, the leader, had developed vertigo and was in quite a state.
>
> I was also affected by the depth. I started laughing. It was a 70-metre deep dive circus by the time David arrived. Unaffected, David tried easing the vertigo by getting Mark to focus on his finger as he moved it slowly back and forth. No success. David saw I was affected and incapable of assisting. Clamping onto Mark's wrist, David towed him at speed back towards the bow. Amused, I followed.
>
> Our leader, Mark, started to recover at about 55-metres depth.
>
> To this day, he has no recollection of being at the stern of the USS *President Coolidge* on that dive. If David hadn't turned up, he'd probably still be there.
>
> – Malcolm Chapman,
retired diving instructor,
October 2017

That first course I did taught me many skills that today would be learned over two, three or even four courses. Some of the skills I learned on that first course aren't taught at all any more, and that's a mistake.

I was also fortunate that my instructors took a shine to me – maybe because they weren't used to anyone passing their course! Before I was fifteen years old, I was helping them run their classes. I was kind of a useful mascot. I would swim the buoys and various equipment into place and escort students between instructors. I was far too young to actually teach, but I was humorously and affectionately referred to as the 'advanced diving provisional assistant instructor'.

As a consequence, the two instructors became somewhat like big brothers and I got to go diving in lots of adventurous places that in those days were really quite out of the way. On those occasions, it would be rare to ever spot a diver outside our little group, or a non-diver for that matter.

Sometimes we would camp. I don't recommend diving and camping – a scuba tank doesn't make a good pillow and you're salty for days, no fresh water, crusty sleeping bags, climbing into salty wetsuits in the cold of a winter's morning by campfire! I'm tensing up at the thought of the discomfort, but as a teenager it was great; I loved it. It was in stark contrast to a few years later when I was guiding groups on international diving holidays and would awaken in my hotel to breakfast via room service before wandering down to the bus to be taken to the dive boat.

In 1972 I received a call from a father who asked me if scuba diving would be personally rewarding and would encourage responsibility and perhaps even develop focus for a teenager who was having difficulty with the relevance of his school curriculum. The father was Bill Oldfield and the teenager was his wild son, David.

I was a school teacher at the time and I understood the disconnect that might be felt between the laws of science, algebra, and life. Especially for a boy such as David who always needed to see a practical purpose in what he was expected to learn. Diving gave David the reason he needed to bother. He soon mastered the role of maths and science in a diving context. The laws and theories of Boyle, Dalton, Henry, Archimedes and Amontons were soon second nature to him.

Naturally, during diver training and associated excursions we sat around beaches, campfires and accommodation common rooms and discussed (mostly debated) a multitude of topics other than those associated with diving. Those present, including my father (a WW II vet), marvelled at David's depth of general knowledge and history subjects including WW II, how weapons worked and the politics behind the Vietnam War, which was still raging at the time. His communication and debating skills were subsequently sharpened amongst people many times his age.

> Diving was very good for David. He experienced amazing things, went on to be one of the youngest dive instructors and instructor examiners ever certified, owned successful diving businesses and eventually became the Australian National Scuba Diving Champion.
>
> – Terry Cummins,
> Australian founder of the Professional Association of Diving Instructors,
> recently retired vice president and head of marketing, PADI Worldwide

The diverse diving experiences aside, from a very early age I was seeing people in physically and psychologically difficult situations – I was witnessing firsthand how people react under duress. Note, 'react'. I have been trying to teach my sons about responding rather than reacting. In all things we must be considered in our approach; we must think and then respond. Reactions often occur without thought, or without enough thought! Easier said than done – especially for humans, most of whom are controlled and consumed by their emotions.

Watching people cope with being hellishly frightened, and in the case of blokes, trying to hide their fear and then afterwards making extraordinary excuses for themselves because they were embarrassed, started me on the path to learning about a whole range of human dysfunctions.

Recreational diving is meant to be undertaken in pairs. It's called the buddy system and the idea is you are mutually responsible for each other's safety. You are meant to know where your buddy is at all times – never lose sight of each other and always be close enough to help in an emergency.

In 1981 I got my friend David Ettridge to come along on a deep wreck dive. David was buddied up with a very experienced deep and wreck diver. David Ettridge notes here how that turned out:

> Around 1979 I joined a Sydney scuba diving club where I met a young David Oldfield. A couple of years later he asked if I'd like to try a deep dive on the wreck of the *Dee Why*, a former Manly ferry. On that dive and at a depth of 150 feet (45 metres) I ran out of air from my single

tank. In the emergency, I swam to find David who, having sensed and then seen I was in difficulty, responded immediately.

David's competence, diving experience and detailed knowledge of decompression requirements saved me that day as we slowly rose to the surface and at the correct depth stages, we stopped and decompressed.

– David Ettridge,
November 2017

Unfortunately, David Ettridge's buddy was too busy with his movie camera and not paying appropriate attention to David. David had done a lot of dives, but other than his original training course, most of those dives had occurred in warm, ideal conditions. I considered him a calm, competent diver, but the depth and cold led to exertion, which led to increased respiration, stress and the increased impact of nitrogen narcosis (sometimes called underwater drunkenness), which quickly turned into an out-of-air situation.

Problems when diving escalate in seconds if not immediately addressed. At 150 feet (45 metres) all issues are amplified, especially so by the combination of stress and the effects of nitrogen narcosis. David Ettridge had plenty of air for the dive, as planned, but matters as described above caused him to drain his air supply at about three times the rate expected. His buddy was otherwise occupied as if he was diving on his own and David naturally turned to me, who he knew well, rather than his own buddy, who remained unaware of the whole drama.

I was wearing separately rigged tanks, that is, two tanks joined in a frame but each independent of the other and each with their own regulator (mouthpiece) and air gauge.

The air supply system I used was the best way to be equipped for what is referred to as a ceilinged environment dive, where circumstances prevent the diver from being able to ascend directly to the surface. Such is the case where something impedes direct access. This may be because you're in a wreck or a cave and must first exit the enclosed space before being able to ascend, or in the case of the aforementioned dive, because we needed to stop on the way up to decompress.

In this case, the impediment to direct access to the surface was that going straight to the surface, without staging stops at specific depths, would lead to the diver suffering decompression sickness. I won't get into details of that, but suffice to say, decompression sickness is never good. It may lead to paralysis and in the very worst case, death. It is often referred to as the bends. I've had it twice and I don't recommend the experience, though both times did teach me things!

With the emergency involving David Ettridge, there was the added difficulty that we were about 40 metres from the anchor line. That might not sound like very far, but underwater, at 45 metres (150 feet) in an out-of-air situation, it's a long way.

The separately rigged twin-tank system I was using is intended essentially to negate the need of help from someone else in an air-supply emergency.The idea is to breathe a predetermined amount from one tank and then switch and breath the same from the other tank.

For example, use a quarter of one tank and then a quarter of the other and keep swapping back and forth so each tank always holds a good proportion of your total air supply. As part of an overall plan, should there be a problem with one tank, your other tank would always have enough air to get you out of trouble without needing the help of another diver – if you had planned appropriately.

It's always best not to have to need assistance because it automatically endangers the helper. Danger is further multiplied substantially by depth, darkness or being inside a wreck, a cave or anything else that complicates immediate access to the surface.

Specialised diving requires very particular planning. Air needs are dealt with through extra equipment and emergency supplies. Calculations always start with the knowledge of your individual air consumption rate. In saying that, many people undertake highly specialised dives inadequately equipped and they think that's fine, until something goes wrong, then they live or die, mostly depending on their level of luck on the day.

I gave David Ettridge one of my regulators (air supply mouthpiece), checked his gauge and noted his tank wasn't quite empty, but with all the stress and his heavy rate of breathing it was low enough to give him the feeling he was effectively out of air.

We swam along the deck of the shipwreck to the anchor line and started a careful ascent, me with one hand hanging on to David and the other maintaining contact with the anchor line.

Ascending in these circumstances is further complicated by the need to let air out of your BCD, otherwise, as you go up, the air in the BCD will proportionally expand and try to drag you uncontrollably to the surface. Staying neutrally buoyant isn't a big deal normally, but in this case, I needed to not only take care of myself, but also maintain contact with the line and look after David to ensure his BCD didn't overinflate and drag him away. This meant looping my elbow around the line with my BCD dump in that hand and my other hand in control of David. He was concentrating on breathing. He wasn't in a state of panic (a whole new ballgame), but he was understandably stressed.

About 18 metres (60 feet) from the surface, we crossed over onto the line that would guide us to steel bars hanging under the boat. This was particularly tricky because it is a light line meant only as a guide between the anchor line and the spot directly beneath the boat, rigged for decompression stops.

This is where being neutrally buoyant becomes even more critical: if you're heavy you pull the line towards the bottom, and if you're buoyant you pull the line, and hence yourself, to the surface. With just yourself to worry about, again, no big deal, but hauling a person out of air and controlling your buoyancy and theirs, requires extra attention to detail, to say the least.

We made it. As soon as we reached the first of the steel bar decompression stops 6 metres (20 feet) below the boat, I switched David from my scuba tank to the emergency air tank attached to the bar. From the time on the shipwreck when I put him onto my air supply to the relative safety of the first decompression stop and the emergency air tank would have only been five to six minutes. When I looked at the pressure gauge on my tank that David Ettridge had been using, it was close to empty. In his stressed high-respiration state, he'd used about twenty-five minutes worth of air in around five minutes.

We completed our two decompression stops and carefully climbed into the boat. Never exert yourself after a dive – especially a deep dive

– best to be relaxed and approach things comfortably and carefully. A good lesson for life, not just diving.

I didn't immediately think too much about what had happened. I'd been on a lot of dives most people would consider risky or dangerous, so I'd experienced and witnessed quite a few things go wrong. At the time, what happened with David was the sort of thing that came with the territory. I tended to just deal with stuff, mostly without surprise, and just get through what I needed to get done.

Later, however, as I sat down to think the emergency through, I considered how it could have been avoided. I was always thinking issues through and looking at what went wrong and how I might decrease the chances of the same situation happening again.

In this specific case, there were matters that, prior to the dive, could have been addressed. That tends to generally be the case. Most 'accidents', are the culmination of a series of human errors, sometimes very subtle errors, and other times glaring errors.

I'm not just talking about diving here; this is true of all things that go wrong, but it was through diving that I learned this all-important lesson. Humans, however, tend not to be very embracing of fault, blame or accepting much in the way of contributory negligence. I tell my sons that the use of the word 'accident' is commonly associated with those who, knowingly or not, are distancing themselves from their mistakes. Equally, in almost all things, there are exceptions, but when human error and or contributory negligence are properly taken into account, accidents, where humans aren't responsible wholly, or at least partially, are so rare as to almost be non-existent.

The accident/incident with David Ettridge was dealt with as well as it could have been. As far as emergency response and lifesaving actions are concerned, it was a 100 per cent positive outcome. But you should only consider your ability to cope with emergencies as a last resort. The best approach is not so much to be the best at fixing things but, rather, being the best at making sure they don't get broken. I hope it's clear again that I'm not just talking diving, but how to treat life as a whole.

There is a view that if the danger is diminished, then so is the adventure, but that is the stuff of morons who make the mistake of thinking the adventure is the danger. Adventures often present dangers, but if it's the danger that gets you off, so to speak, you may as well stay at home in comfort and play Russian roulette – all danger, no actual adventure, and, over time, a bad result is assured. Though I suppose, if you subscribe to the stupid in the world carrying out a means of self-eradication, then you may not see it as an entirely bad result.

Sensible adventuring, if I may call it that, is where you have a sustainable reason to do something that is potentially dangerous, but where you use knowledge, planning, preparation and associated equipment to reduce the danger, so the risk is logically countered and diminished. Something really dangerous can't be made 100 per cent safe, but you can likely get a lot of activities down to 99 per cent safe and know you can reasonably deal with the other 1 per cent if the shit hits the fan. Know what you're doing, understand the implications, know you're capable of doing it, have a plan, be prepared and practiced, be appropriately equipped and have backup to deal with contingencies. If you're involving yourself in dangerous activities and not doing these things, then you're back playing Russian roulette.

Many people make mistakes that could have been fatal and instead of examining where things went wrong, attributing blame, learning the lesson and considering how the mistake could have been avoided, they bash on with the absurd notion luck prevailed, or that some skill they think they have rescued them. Much of that can be put down to *ego*! We humans, for the most part seem not to want to admit errors to ourselves, let alone have someone else know we screwed up.

This serious human personality disorder is such that some consider laying blame elsewhere to be a skill, and maybe for climbing the corporate ladder or just keeping your job, that may be true, but when physical danger is a component, it's best to keep those people far away. I'd suggest this predominantly relates to men – certainly so in the area of 'death defying feats'.

I learned as a young diving instructor that ego often stands in the way of learning and I made up a little saying that I passed on to students on specialised diving courses:

'Ego is the door that closes itself to learning.' I thought it so succinct and profound. Not because it's mine, but because it so simply encapsulates the whole scenario of how an unwillingness to accept blame leads to an inability to learn from mistakes and hence reduce the prospect of making the same mistakes again.

Unfortunately, given my well-meaning naivety, it was quite some time before it dawned on me that the people who'd most benefit from this were, by nature, those most likely to be unable to learn its lesson. How does one teach an egotist anything? Anyway, the thought was there and what I was trying to teach had a good impact on those who were less egotistical and able to appreciate the need to examine their own actions and the roles they played in things that went wrong.

It will come as no surprise that years after my diving career was behind me, I found politics and the media to have much more than its share of egomaniacs. I discovered to my horror (naivety again) that in those fields, anyone who knew something others didn't was seen as a threat, not a source of information.

Perhaps you've seen this in your own area, but the macho nature of diving and the ambitious nature of media and politics seem to attract that kind in disproportionate numbers. Perhaps this is just how people are everywhere in every field.

Furthering how the experience of diving teaches so many lessons for life, I can't help but return to the day David Ettridge came close to losing his life. It's an important lesson because even when you succeed you should examine why that occurred – success shouldn't be taken for granted as to how it takes place. The rescue of David Ettridge was a great success and for a lot of people that's where it would end, but as you've probably picked up, for me, there are few situations that occur truly by accident, or through plain bad luck.

What was wrong with the organisation of the dive on which David Ettridge had his brush with death? In the first instance, there is an argument that David shouldn't have been on the dive. That's an easy answer, though for the most part not entirely apparent until after the dive. David Ettridge had done more than fifty dives – there were instructors with only that much experience under their belts. By the way, I know that isn't enough experience to realistically be teaching scuba diving, but that's another story.

David's experience was reasonably diverse – he'd done shore dives, boat dives, wreck dives, night dives and he'd dived close to the same depth before. All in all, he was a fairly experienced diver. David was, and is, a calm, intelligent and considered man, not prone to outbursts, and he is a teetotaller. All of this generally rings well for deep diving; however, his experience on dives over 30 metres (100 feet) was almost exclusively in tropical conditions – warm, clear water.

It was a calm clear day and underwater visibility was good, about 18 metres (60 feet) horizontally on the wreck, but it was colder than David was accustomed to and the descent from a small boat was a different experience to that which he was accustomed.

Descending to depth on a long angle, down an anchor line, on an average winter's day on a wreck off Sydney can seem as if you are descending into darkness, and if it's something you haven't done before it would likely lead to an element of trepidation.

Then there is the matter of nitrogen narcosis. This is a narcotic feeling brought about by the increased partial pressure (Dalton's Law – google it) of the gas nitrogen. It's always there, but commonly becomes more apparent in divers over 30 metres (100 feet) and it's always a potential issue when using compressed air. Nitrogen narcosis can be removed by simply removing the nitrogen in your gas mix and substituting helium, but this is generally too much mucking around for most divers.

Most scuba diving is undertaken with the use of compressed air – essentially just what we all breathe every day – so nitrogen narcosis can only be dealt with through experience, acclimatisation, focus, fitness and concentration. Deep diving isn't for dummies and or those with poor attention span.

I've functioned very well in depths over 75 metres (246 feet) and on my deepest dive, I hit 100 metres (328 feet) though I wouldn't recommend trying that on compressed air as I did.

Mmmm, nitrogen narcosis. Most divers have no idea how badly it debilitates them until they are called upon to perform a seemingly easy task.

Divers must take care in planning dives in a fashion that maximises averting problems and doesn't rely on memory because, once at depth, the capacity to deal with emergencies is very seriously diminished and for a lot of divers the capacity to remember instructions is largely gone.

So should David Ettridge have been on the dive? As I suggested earlier, it's easier to answer that after the out-of-air emergency than before the dive. Hindsight is a wonderful thing, but the skill is developing the capacity to look ahead at all the variables and avoid the problems. For the most part, David's capacity to deal with this dive was apparent and positive, so it isn't as easy as just saying he shouldn't have been on the dive. The main problem here was the person David was buddied with; his partner in misadventure was a very experienced deep diver, but somewhat of a loner who was more interested in his movie camera than David.

Knowing he was buddied with someone who hadn't done a dive quite like this before, his partner should have been paying more attention, but once they hit the wreck, with a little nitrogen narcosis in the mix for the pair of them, his focus switched 100 per cent to filming. David was left to follow his buddy who was seeing the whole dive through the viewfinder of his movie camera – not an effective operation of the buddy system.

David Ettridge was a bit cold, a bit stressed and those two things increase respiration and together they further increase the effects of nitrogen narcosis. David was chewing through his air and his state impeded him from properly monitoring what was happening to him and his air supply. It's the old 'snowballing effect', the longer you go on oblivious to your plight, the worse it becomes. The faster you breathe, the colder you get and the colder you get, the faster you breathe. The stress builds and there you have it – in less than half of the planned time on the bottom, David is close to being out of air and starting to find breathing difficult.

His partner, however, is up ahead, in his own little world, filming the wreck and completely unaware his buddy is in strife. David knows he's in trouble and is looking around, clearly stressed, and unable to do much for himself. At the same time, I'm kind of swimming top cover, watching out for everyone, and I spot David is in trouble as he spots me. We got to each other and it all ended well.

Buddies should show each other their gauges, so each diver knows things are on track regarding air consumption in relation to time. It's supposed to be a continual process, but most divers wait till they're low on air before indicating the level of their supply.

If David had been my buddy, there wouldn't have been an emergency. I naturally stay on top of how much air my buddy has. It doesn't matter who it is or how experienced they are, I've been watching over other divers since I was fourteen so I couldn't have helped but check their air – it was what I did.

I'm still like that now, but it's not air, it's everything – I naturally make sure those around me are okay. If I'm bushwalking, I make sure people are keeping up, I call the breaks and I check on everyone's water; that's who I am. I'm pretty sure diving made me that way.

See that's it, diving is really quite dangerous. You are in an utterly alien environment relying for your life on a tank of air and associated equipment. The deeper you are, or the more complex the environment (night, shipwreck, cave), the more dangerous it is, and that's a fact.

Don't get me wrong, diving is amazing and beautiful and an extraordinary adventure, but it's other world stuff and you're not meant to be there. Don't let some New Age numb-nut convince you you're one with the ocean or any similar hippie bullshit, because you're not.

That said, the dangers can be mitigated almost completely, but not entirely. You can train and be experienced and careful and have all the best gear, but it's still dangerous and if you have to help somebody else down there, they may kill you as well as themselves.

I don't want that to seem overly dramatic, but it is a fact that diving equipment manufacturers and diving schools don't tend to acknowledge because it's bad for business. Beginners mostly survive because the equipment is generally excellent, they're not diving deep and nothing goes wrong. The real test of how good a diver you are is what you manage to do when things go wrong.

The trouble is, when it comes to people, almost anything can happen and just like driving a car, you might be the safest driver on the road, but someone else could do something that couldn't have reasonably been taken into account.

Maybe you know someone killed by a drunk in another car – I do. I also knew a fellow crippled for life because a car coming down a hill jumped the middle section of the road into his car as he was going up the same hill.

Believe me, it's best to never have something go wrong on a scuba dive – especially a dive where depth is a component, and or, also involving a closed ceilinged environment such as a cave or a shipwreck. Bottom line, when the shit hits the fan you will be able to rely on almost no-one at all, but that will likely not be completely apparent until it's too late.

Are you asking whether we're still talking diving? Good point, and the answer is yes, we're still talking diving, and every other single facet of life as well – beware of whom you rely on! Yep, diving is vastly more dangerous than anyone selling diving gear will ever mention!

That's not to say you shouldn't go diving; not at all in any sense am I suggesting that, but the fact is you will be in an alien environment which is like being on another planet and just the most wonderful thing, until something goes wrong.

Diving is adventurous and then some, and the risks are diminished proportionally by training, practice, fitness, preparedness, planning, effective use of equipment and always being in good company.

I loved diving and I loved teaching diving. I went to great lengths to teach others to be the very best divers they could be. I was born by the ocean and was very water-oriented from the start. I was organising dives for others at eighteen, a qualified instructor and a partner in my first dive shop at twenty-one and I was leading international diving tours to the some of the best locations in the world – life was good.

When I qualified as a Master Diving Instructor, I was one of only eight in Australia and I was the youngest by a long way. By the time I was twenty-eight, I owned three dive shops, I'd been captain of the New South Wales state scuba diving team and been the Australian

Open Diving Champion as well as the National Underwater Photography Champion.

Around this time, I'd also become the New South Wales Coaching Director for the Australian Underwater Federation (the government-recognised administrator of the sport of diving) and later moved on to be the chairman of the Federal Technical Committee. Among other things, this meant I represented Australia at international scuba diving conferences convened by the world body and I compiled information on the root causes of diving accidents, most specifically, deaths. I taught almost every type of diving there was and focused especially on the types of diving that required the most concentration and skill: deep diving, wreck diving, cavern and cave diving.

At my peak, I was diving 500 times a year and on occasion would spend sixteen hours in a wetsuit in a single day, teaching four separate and different classes. I was a busy boy, particularly through my twenties. I ate, breathed and slept diving seemingly twenty-four hours a day. In one four-year period in the 1980s I worked seven days a week and generally four nights, teaching, lecturing, coordinating divers and selling equipment. During those four years, the only days off I had were Christmas Day and Good Friday, because they were the only days the dive shops were closed. I loved it. For a long time I didn't think I would ever do anything else! Clearly, I was wrong.

Do I want my sons to dive? Actually, no, I wouldn't encourage it, but if they want to learn, I'll make sure of what they learn, and I wouldn't be keen on them diving without me. I now understand my mother's concerns when I would mention I was off to teach a class, and she would say, 'Be careful son.'

I remember once saying to her, 'Mum, I'm twenty-eight years old, I'm a Master Diving Instructor and an Australian champion and I'm going to be in 6 metres of water teaching – what do you think is going to happen?'

Mum said, 'Just be careful son.' She was right, you can never be too careful.

So what do you think, should David Ettridge have been on that dive?

The answer is yes, but not with the buddy he had. I should have buddied with him. For all the experience his buddy had, he was a hell of a loner and a terrible buddy. That I let the two of them go together means I'm somewhat to blame. I thought I had things covered by acting as an overall safety diver with eyes on the whole picture to a degree, and it was because of that I was positioned to save David. It wasn't my responsibility as such, I was just on the dive like everybody else, but I should have stepped in. Had I thought it through appropriately, I would have been with David from the start and my natural propensity to constantly check everything would have prevented the emergency from ever happening.

Some of you might think I'm being a little hard on myself, but it's only by being hard on yourself that lessons are forever remembered; indeed, that lessons are even learned in the first place. Be hard on yourself and those you love. Better to be prepared and not need it, than to need it and not be prepared – you'll all be better off in the end and especially so, when 'the shit hits the fan'. And be assured, it will.

David in Politics

I couldn't have told you a time as a child when I ever imagined being a politician, but strangely, when my dad died, and I was clearing out his garage (a horrible time), I found a box of old exercise books from first year high school – I was under age, so eleven at the time. In one of the books there was a list of things I wanted to do when I 'grew up'. In clear bold print, there it was, 'politician'. To add to the craziness, listed with politician, there was also 'diving instructor' and 'radio announcer'.

This was in 2008. By then, I'd been a politician and a diving instructor and I'd just a few months before, started my career on radio. Sometimes I tell myself I've already done all the things I planned as a child and sometimes I wonder what that leaves that is yet to be done, other than to guide, nurture and love my sons.

In 1989, I was pretty carefree, though working hard seven days a week in my diving business, and that was okay, as diving was my life in those days – I ate, drank and slept diving, which is difficult as you're wet most of the time. When I wasn't out in the water teaching, I was selling in the store or unpacking stock or lecturing students in one of the classrooms. If I had a day off, I didn't know what else to do, so for the most part I didn't have days off.

When something so absorbs your whole life, you tend not to notice a lot outside of your own activities and that's pretty much where I was at when my local council started to look at banning diving from all the local beaches. I was terribly naive to think that couldn't happen. I was born in the suburb of Manly and had lived there my whole life. It was the base of my main business – how on earth could anyone think they could just tell us we were no longer allowed to operate?

It wouldn't be inaccurate to suggest my town council had been infiltrated by what we Manly locals referred to as 'blow-ins'. There was a new block on the council made up of people who'd recently moved to the area and were set on lots of changes.

It was something I didn't understand; if the place was so good you wanted to move here, why are you suddenly trying to change everything? Little did I know that question would have so much to do with how a lot of my politics would be shaped in the years to come.

I discovered this new group had gatherings once a week where ratepayers/residents, could address them about issues prior to the formal council meetings where the decisions would be made, so I booked myself in and off I went. I explained my case to this foursome of strangers who apparently wielded such supreme local power, and was shocked to find they weren't interested at all. They had an agenda and they didn't give a stuff how it impacted anyone, my livelihood included.

There'd been the matter raised that it was hard for locals to park at the beaches because all the parking was taken up by divers. This was, of course, a nonsense, as divers wouldn't have accounted for 1 per cent of people visiting Manly beaches, but the divers were clearly identifiable because of their gear. This new group on council weren't silly when it came to understanding the ugly nature of playing politics. They reasoned they could further their local support by scapegoating divers as the parking culprits and be seen to be addressing the issue directly with a total ban on diving.

At that time, it was hard for me to comprehend how something so unfair was happening, or that people like this existed – that they could be so utterly without concern for the innocents they would impact through their plan to ultimately take complete control of the town council. As I stood to leave, or rather, as I was essentially being dismissed by these people who had just told me they were about to ruin my life, I looked at them and said, 'I'm going to run for council at the next election and I'm going to stop you.'

They looked at me curiously, half smirking, half laughing, and insincerely wished me luck. They were right; what was I going to do? Me, the young naive local dive shop owner. As if I was going to thwart their agenda.

Except they were wrong! Tony Abbott, just a few years later, described me as 'indefatigable'. Not so much these days, but back then, I was single, no kids or animals and my only responsibility was to my business. Back then, I was strong and aggressive, and I didn't know anything about the filth of politics, but I was tough – I'd nearly been killed lots of times and survived some crazy things and I wasn't much for being messed with. Back then, I had a willingness to fight that never gave up and I never backed down – all of these things are to a degree signs of too much testosterone, but that was helpful at the time.

In the short term, I had enough influence to get to the ears of the majority of councillors and I slowed the evil plan, but I knew it was only a matter of time, so I did what I told them I'd do – at the next election, I ran for council.

It's kind of 'no interest like self-interest', but the reality was that even though the ban would have made life difficult, it wouldn't have been impossible. The greatest motivating factor for me was how awful I considered this pack who'd moved in on my town. Yes, I was that naive! I truly believed the good guys wore white hats, the cavalry were always right and the Indians were always murdering savages, and I was about to set out to right some wrongs.

In reality, it's kind of nice to live your life without ever having to deal with dirt, rather than being forced to face that nothing is as it seems; it would be great to stay that innocent and not be impacted by other people's garbage.

I didn't know about running for election, but I understood marketing, sales and promotion and I did a bit of reading and I introduced myself to people who'd been at politicking for years.

It was 1991 and the election was due in September. In those days, no-one my age got elected to council. Manly council had been dominated by middle-aged to elderly business people and community workers – a young dive shop owner who looked like he might not yet be shaving didn't stand a chance. People already on the council who were running for re-election saw me as a means to help them; rather than being concerned about me actually getting elected, everyone wanted my preferences.

One particular wannabe, who'd been trying and failing for years, though considered himself an expert, specifically told me, 'You can't get elected – nobody gets elected the first time they run, but with your preferences, I can win and then I'll help you next time.'

Like I said, I didn't understand politics, but I had always been good with numbers. I looked at previous results, studied preference flows and determined the likely number of primary votes to place me where I needed to be for preferences to get me over the line. I hooked up with a former mayor and her running mate and did a deal where I would run third on their ticket, but I would hand out my own how-to-votes in which I placed myself at number one and them at two and three. The maths of it was that I needed to have enough primary votes to push past the fellow running second, in front of me, on the former mayor's ticket, so I would then get his preferences. It was impossible, or so the experts thought – no one had tried it before!

As I was saying, I hadn't been in a campaign before, but I knew what sells and I knew how to sell myself. I targeted issues in individual streets – simple things like potholes and kerbing and guttering. This was before direct mail, so it was innovative of me to write letters addressed to residents in specific streets where I'd identified problems, and then put those letters, not in their letterboxes, but under their front doors – that hadn't been done before either.

Instead of thinking my apparent youthfulness to be a negative, I promoted it as a positive. I had a nice portrait photograph in which I probably looked about twenty-five and I circulated that with slogans including, 'a fresh face for Manly', and 'new blood for Manly Council'.

Between family and friends, we manned all the polling booths in the electorate thanks to my mother, who drew up a schedule and allocated people to the polling places to hand out my how-to-vote cards. Clearly I did enough right, as I substantially outpolled the fellow I did the deal with on the former mayor's ticket and, as predicted, his and other preferences flowed to me.

In classic fashion, as the preferences on election night continued to trickle to me in the count, the final few that put me over the line came from the 'expert' who'd told me, in no uncertain terms, that I couldn't get elected, but my preferences would help him.

And so it began. I was elected as an alderman (later councillor) to Manly Council. The poor council officers and the administration were not prepared for someone not acquainted with the genteel behaviour of council – they weren't used to someone who'd say what they really thought. Still, everyone had to make do, as is often the case when public servants are saddled with elected people who don't fit the mould and generally don't fall in line. I grew to respect many of those administrators and do so still today.

I made quite an impression on my local community – I was brash and outspoken and I garnered many headlines and didn't take shit from anyone, but I genuinely tried to help those who deserved support and I generally succeeded in the interests of the residents I represented.

I also succeeded in stopping the council from banning diving and although I had to declare an interest, I was integral in ultimately supporting a licensing system that was reasonable and affordable for local business, my own included.

I'd gotten into politics for the right reason, to stop things that were unfair, that were wrong. It had taken people trying to do something to me for me to see the need to do something, but the result was I was pushed to do the right thing.

As had often been the case, I'd impressed people, but I made a lot of enemies at the same time. There were those wanting to stop me because they opposed my views and there were the others who wanted to stop me because I was competition for their own political ambitions.

At the end of 1993, the Liberal Party preselected me to be their candidate for the coming state election. It was said to be the dirtiest preselection the New South Wales Liberals had ever seen; though not through anything I did, but because of what was done to stop me.

Unfortunately, I'd wandered into the path of another person's long-held ambition to be the parliamentarian for the Manly electorate. This person had for years worked towards the moment when they would seal the deal and become the member for Manly and I'd gotten in the way. He'd been on every conceivable community committee, been the head of this and the head of that and been the deputy mayor and the president of Manly Rugby Club and I'd stepped in his way.

I'd been put through every conceivable allegation and been forced to clear myself of spurious and ridiculous claims every step of the way, but I'd made it and defeated him in the selection process. But it didn't end there.

The preselection for Manly was the earliest in the state – seventeen months before the election. The seat was held by the most recognisable independent in New South Wales and it was felt the Liberal candidate would need a long campaign to have any chance to win. Once I'd won the preselection, I then went through nearly a year and a half of upheaval because the other candidate and his backers wouldn't accept the decision. They undermined me and did all they could to have me dismissed, so their candidate could step in and take my place.

In the closing weeks of the campaign, when there was no opportunity to have me replaced, when all their dirty tactics had failed, they then started to undermine the campaign itself. Call it naivety again, but it was beyond my belief. They preferred I lose the election and the independent win again because then their candidate would no doubt be given the chance in four years' time. If I were to win and defeat this independent the Liberals so detested, it would have been near impossible to take that away from me and my rival would never have gotten what he already considered his as if by some birthright.

On election day, some 'Liberals' didn't turn up to staff the polling booths, so a few places went hours without 'How to Vote Liberal' material being available – that hurt! Of course, they did all they could behind the scenes to stop people voting for me by running the quiet campaign of 'even his own party don't want him to win'. A lot of it wasn't all that quiet, though, as I suffered many stories along those lines in the media in the build-up to election day.

On election night, it went down to the wire. After recounts, it took over a week to finalise the result: I lost – the independent was re-elected. Had around a 100 of the 47,000 voters changed their vote, it would have changed the result and I'd have become the member for Manly.

> I can't recall ever meeting a more focused and indefatigable candidate. No-one in my experience has given so much of himself to a cause he believes in and a goal he desperately wanted to achieve.
>
> – The Honourable Tony Abbott MP,
> parliamentary secretary and Federal Member for Warringah,
> May 1997

It was the closest election result in New South Wales and it was as if my life had been ended. I don't think I had ever been so low. I fell into a deep depression. To have been so robbed; to have been so mistreated and all because of the ambitions of one fellow who couldn't beat me by the rules – I was still a little naive and still thinking that good guys wore white hats. Oh, and I was still thinking there were rules – silly me.

I'd sold my business to personally fund myself as a full-time candidate for the election, such was my commitment. Now there was just me, the four walls of my apartment and no feeling of wanting to do anything or even talk to anyone.

I'm not proud of what happened to me, but it is what it is, and this is about how I am – I started to drink. I didn't leave my apartment for days at a time. I would heat up a frozen quiche and sit in front of the TV and drink from a wine cask – the good stuff, you know, the 2-litre variety not the 4-litre ones!

It was a decidedly ugly time. I wouldn't say I became an alcoholic as such, but I was certainly self-medicating my woes. Alcohol is the cure, not the disease, and in this case, it was helping me through each night of my self-imposed solitude. I think it really was more about how I cut myself off from everything rather than the drinking. I was so broken, so embarrassed, though through it all, each week, I got myself together and attended my town council meeting – yep, I was still a councillor.

To the outside world, there was nothing apparent, because although I was bottled up in my apartment, I seemed to still be around and functioning, as my council work was very public, so only my parents noticed anything was amiss.

I'm staying relatively brief about the eight months or so that I essentially retired from life because I expect you get the idea. I was still in this crazy kind of control, just not living in any normal sense. But I didn't turn to drugs or do anything illegal and still managed to exert a level of willpower. No matter how much it has seemed like I wanted to or should, I've never been able to ever fully give up.

Some of you might conclude what I later did in leaving Tony Abbott and creating One Nation was some sort of payback – a desire for revenge would be eminently understandable given what was done to me and all those supporting me, merely so one man might fulfil his ambitions. However, I didn't hold it against the Liberal Party. What was done was done by a gang within the Liberal Party, not the party itself. In fact, there were many good people within the party who had campaigned hard for my election and been trusted supporters. It was a minority of ratbags who were responsible – it would have been completely unreasonable to blame the Liberals as a whole. Despite all I've learned, I remain reasonable; indeed, I'm more reasonable now than I was then, though I'm no longer quite as naive.

At the end of 1995, I wasn't showing much in the way of change. I was still, for the most part, locked up and unhappy, but such is my capacity to force myself, that I got out enough to be re-elected to the council, and with four times the votes I'd received at the previous election.

I'd managed that with the help of local people, who remained committed to me. I was so fortunate that even though I was in a form of self-imposed exile from a relatively normal life, there were still people who believed I had something to offer. In the end, it was my dad who initiated what started me on the road to really doing things again. He contacted my cousin in Western Australia and told him how I was and asked if he might suggest I come and visit. My cousin, one of Perth's most successful architects, called me and did exactly that, so I did. Before Christmas of 1995, I was on a plane to Perth.

I will always owe my cousin for his simple yet enormous act of kindness. Without him, I may have gone on for another year; who knows, but that would have cut off a series of opportunities, all of which led me to everything I did that followed.

It's been nearly twenty-five years now and I'm not sure I ever thanked my cousin, Ian, enough. Thinking back on it, despite the appearance of functioning, sometimes at quite a high level (such as during my council re-election campaign), it was as if my head was always spinning.

Ian was well connected in Perth and I spent two weeks with him meeting serious people of substance. They all treated me with decency and respect. They were interested in me and didn't know me for the loser I spent so many nights thinking myself to be. I impressed some high-flyers to the point of being offered jobs, and for a moment or two, moving to Perth seemed a good idea, but in the end, it was too much. Sydney, Manly in particular, was my home and if I was to fix my life, I needed to go home to do it. You can't run away from problems when the problems are inside you, they go with you and stay with you wherever you choose to hide.

David was determined to get the right things done for the people he represented and worked hard for the seat of Manly.

References for him would say he's honest and reliable, but David goes far beyond the writing of those words on paper. He truly is one of those rare people who does what he tells you he's going to do – he fights, often at great personal cost, to make things happen and in 1999, he was elected to the New South Wales State Parliament for an eight-year term.

Given his ability, David deserved greater success, but there was always an undercurrent pulling him down. Is he the victim of our 'tall poppy syndrome'? I think that's likely – I don't know how else to explain why he was continually undermined.

Those who would say David was radical might realise what he

proposed is these days a big part of the landscape. This was evident during his radio broadcasting career.

– John Thorpe AM,
former state and national president of the Australian Hotels Association

In the new year of 1996, the next federal election was soon to be called and Tony Abbott was out on the hustings – I was with him.

Tony and I were, to a degree, separated by allegiances, though not so much by ideology. I'd liked him since meeting him when he paid me a visit in the run-up to when he stood for preselection for the seat of Warringah. At that time, I was already the candidate for Manly and the president of the Manly branch of the Liberal Party. Manly branch was the largest and most financially successful branch in the Warringah electorate. Manly branch also provided the largest number of selectors of any branch. It was fair to say I had a level of influence that Tony wanted to neutralise.

Tony came to convince me not to tell people to vote against him in the preselection for Warringah. It wasn't a hard ask – whenever my opinion on such things was sought, I always suggested voting for the best candidate. In Tony's case, I took that a step further; I told preselectors quite specifically that if they considered Tony the best candidate, then he deserved their vote and they shouldn't let anyone talk them out of that. Had I pushed selectors not to vote for Tony, I suspect the preselection would have gone against him and that would have been wrong, because he was the best candidate – he was in a league of his own.

I did quite a few meet and greets on street corners and in shopping centres with Tony in the lead up to the 1996 election, but when the election was called, I travelled north to help Bob Baldwin in the seat of Paterson. Tony was a shoo-in and had all the help in the world; Bob, however, was in a marginal seat that was held by Labor – it was exactly the sort of seat the Liberals had to win to secure government. Bob has credited me with being instrumental in him winning that seat, which he then sadly lost in 1998, regained in 2001 and held until his retirement in 2016.

> David's management and analytical ability is why I asked David to join me as my campaign director in my 1993 campaign for Dobell and the successful 1996 campaign for Paterson. Though we eventually travelled separate political paths, our friendship has endured over time.
>
> – The Honourable Bob Baldwin MP,
> former parliamentary secretary (assistant minister) and member for Paterson,
> March 2018

After Tony was re-elected in 1996, he was promoted to Parliamentary Secretary (Assistant Minister) to the Minister for Education, Employment, Training and Youth Affairs. It was a huge portfolio and he hired me as his Private Secretary – the story of which is detailed elsewhere in this book.

Despite how politicians carry on about all the differences they make, unless you're a minister, you're not going to make any outstanding difference to much, if anything. A good local member will help individuals in their electorates, but the big items are accomplished by ministers, Cabinet, the premier or prime minister. That's just the way things are – if you don't have a specific area of responsibility, and hence power within a government, there's little you can do. Most of the time in parliament you're just someone to sit on one side of the room or the other in votes for or against legislation. The way the party system of government operates, many MPs and senators don't know what they're voting on – they just sit to be counted with the rest of their side.

As the Liberal candidate for Manly in the 1995 election, however, I did something quite unique and of substantial importance, and I did it as a mere candidate, and such is absolutely unheard of.

Just like my first run for council, some of my campaign for parliament in 1995 was quite groundbreaking. Most particularly, the work I did to stop the reintroduction of dock statements.

What's a dock statement, I hear you ask. This is a statement given in court by lowlife scum, rapists, murderers, paedophiles, for the purpose of improving their lot. It was an unsworn statement without limits and it wasn't subject to any cross-examination. This meant it could be filled with exaggerations and, frankly, downright lies. It was effectively a personal explanation that was never tested before the court. The grubs could say anything they thought might help them without fear of so much as being asked a single thing.

It was loved by criminals and defence lawyers and prisoners' action groups and anyone who for reasons best known to themselves supported the worst of the worst being penalised as minimally as possible or even found not guilty due to perceived mitigating factors. It was, however, very disturbing to victims, if they were still alive, and their families, as they would be forced to sit through unquestioned lies intended to gain sympathy for the accused.

Dock statements in the state of New South Wales had been abolished in 1994, but the independent MP in Manly, who I was up against, had a plan to have them reintroduced. I learned of this when I met a group of people who were the parents of murder victims – in many cases, the victims had been children. When they told me of the plan to reintroduce this heinous practice, I thought it something I should try and stop.

I authored a letter explaining exactly what the independent member had planned and several sets of parents signed the letter with a line explaining the murder of their child. It was dynamite politically. The Liberal Party couldn't believe I'd gained the support of the parents and put it together – there had never before been anything like it and I don't think there's been anything like it since.

The letter was posted by addressed mail to every voter in the Manly electorate. Polling showed its devastating effect; it had been enough on its own to change the outcome of the campaign.

Sadly, I think the Liberal powers that be chose to send the letter about a week too early, so there was an element of time for our opponents to muddy some of the facts, but given the campaign within the Liberal Party to sabotage my election, in the end, it didn't matter. However, it may stand as my best work in politics, and all without being elected at the time, for the letter's impact was so frightening to those pushing to reintroduce dock statements, that the plan was dropped, and to this day, twenty-five years later, has not resurfaced. If I was regarded as having achieved nothing but that alone in politics, all the horror and heartache would still have been worthwhile.

During that 1996–97 period working for Tony Abbott, the fellow for whom my 1995 parliamentary campaign was sabotaged and derailed, was found to have defrauded the trust fund he oversaw in his legal practice, was convicted and did several years in jail. My life had been close to destroyed, the work of so many Liberal supporters and workers dashed, the seat of Manly lost, and all for a person who, had he been the candidate and won, would have been forced from office shortly thereafter.

It's unfortunate, often for many, when the misplaced ambition of the few, or sometimes just one person, does so much damage. In the case of Manly, the closest the Liberals came to winning the seat was with my campaign in 1995 – it wasn't until 2007 that the seat finally returned to the party by a narrow margin.

It's funny in the strangest of ways, considering how different my life nearly was, though not for the first time, due to events so very far beyond my control. Without the sabotage of my first parliamentary campaign, I would most likely have been the Liberal member for Manly, and, given my win over the independent, possibly I'd have been there for quite some time. I wouldn't have met Pauline Hanson, because I would have been a state MP in Sydney, not a staffer in Canberra, and Pauline Hanson's One Nation would never have come to exist.

It's hard to say what would have happened to Pauline, but most likely she'd have stood as an independent for the Senate in 1998, and without a party structure, perhaps only had a small chance of election. She'd have likely disappeared had it not been for the party I created in her name. My apologies: I accept the fact she's still around toying with politics and giving people false hope is, to a degree, my fault. Apart from Pauline, the more than twenty members of parliament elected in her name through the party, the people they beat, and all the roll-on effects of all that and more – well, none of that would have happened either.

More importantly for me, I met my wife Lisa at the airport following a One Nation related flight to Broken Hill – I wouldn't have been on that flight, not been at the airport and not ever met Lisa.

My beautiful boys Henry and Albert wouldn't have been born and my whole life, as a Liberal MP, would have been entirely different to the life I actually did have.

So many lives changed because some bloke thought his personal plan to be the member for Manly was going to be made to happen and nothing was going to stand in the way. Today, when I look into my sons' eyes, I say thank you to that person. If you and your flunkies hadn't done me over in 1995, I wouldn't have these two little sons and they mean far more to me than life itself. If I'd been the Liberal member for Manly, they wouldn't exist, and Lord knows where I would be without them.

So much that might have been and wasn't; instead, my fate was to meet Pauline Hanson and create One Nation, and there is no escaping that was an unbelievably unique time in Australian political history. It was also personally very exciting. I was under the impression I was making a difference in the way I believed I should, and there were bigger things to come.

Following the launch of the party on 11 April 1997 we shortly set off on a series of meetings all over Australia. There was tremendous fervour – people were clamouring to see Pauline in person. They were even paying to do so. We didn't have any money, so we charged admission to hear and meet Pauline – it was merely to cover the enormous expenses of hiring halls and all the related costs. It was $5 or sometimes $10 and while I suspect we were the only political party charging admission, I never heard anyone baulk at paying or ask for a refund. No other politician in Australia would have been able to pull such crowds; it was amazing.

While there were many meetings with 500 to 1000 people in attendance, the standout, in so many ways, was a meeting in Newcastle. It was one of our very first. There were 1500 people in the hall, and an estimated 2000 outside, made up of protestors and spectators, and there were 350 New South Wales and Federal Police surrounding the building to keep the peace and ensure safety. I don't know if politics in Australia had ever seen anything like this – it certainly hasn't happened since. The police had a helicopter on stand-by to take Pauline off from the roof if the protestors broke through the barricades.

Yes, exciting unforgettable times with potential beyond belief. I truly thought we were on our way to changing Australia.

The first electoral test for the new party was the Queensland state election held in June 1998. However, there is one event I must squeeze in here because it got One Nation back on track, was history making itself, and carried us through to that first election. That is the Pauline Hanson video, 'If you're seeing me now, it's because I've been murdered'. Like a lot of things I did, it was enormously controversial and the first of its kind.

Pauline hated this video – she still talks about how embarrassed she was by all the other parliamentarians and many in the media attacking her for making it. It clearly never dawned on Pauline that all those people hated that she made it because it worked! When your enemies hate something and attack you over it, it's usually because they see you've been advantaged. One must always be sceptical of criticism from the opposition – it's never well-meaning.

In November of 1997, Pauline Hanson's One Nation was on the ropes – it was all but over. From polls giving us 12 and 13 per cent, we'd collapsed to 3 per cent and there wasn't anything looking like changing that. Pauline had shunned the media for months and that made the party reactive rather than proactive. There was no interest in us. It was a continuous downhill slide. I had to find a way to put Pauline, and hence the party, back in the news.

Pauline had always been subject to a huge level of threat. She received the most horrible anonymous descriptions of how she and her family would be tortured and killed. It was a genuine issue assessed by ASIO and as such she had a full-time team of armed special federal agents assigned to her. Pauline's house in Queensland had substantial security installed and there were armed federal police on duty there 24/7. ASIO even swept my apartment in Sydney for bugs, such was the level of danger to Pauline.

It occurred to me that we could draw a lot of attention and support if people were made aware of what Pauline was being subjected to because of her quest to 'save Australia'. I knew by then Pauline couldn't save stamps, but it was all about portraying a believable image.

I came up with a plan to be clear beyond doubt that Pauline was a courageous fighter, under threat, unconcerned for her own safety, and what the nation must do should something happen to her. I approached Channel Seven and put a simple plan to them. They would film a video of Pauline, scripted by me, where Pauline would disclose to the nation the threat she was under and the need for her supporters to go forward even more strongly without her, should she, indeed, be murdered.

I explained they could do a program on the threat to Pauline's life and the fact it was so real she'd made a 'from beyond the grave' style video to urge Australians not to give up the fight. The deal was they put to air a program highlighting the dangers Pauline faced – Australia's most threatened politician ever – and in return, they had the full video for an exclusive should one of the awful threats be carried out. Channel Seven could use an appropriate snippet of the video in the program and therefore demonstrate a complete version actually did exist.

Whether anything happened or not to Pauline, this was going to be unique, absolutely unique, and a huge story, but the producer I spoke to didn't really get the extraordinary nature of this piece of television I was offering them. Perhaps it was so strange and foreign to her that she just couldn't grasp its potential, but her superiors at Channel Seven certainly caught on straight away!

From when she left me to when I received the call to say yes, yes, yes, when can we start, was about the time it would have taken her to drive back to the station to brief her boss – they'd clearly decided immediately.

When the show went to air, it was as if the roof had collapsed on Australian politics – no-one had seen anything like this and the political classes couldn't believe it. Essentially, it was such an idea 'out of left field', that the reaction was just one of shock. They'd never seen this type of thing or considered anything like this could happen, so no-one had anything in their playbook as to how to deal with it.

For the previous twenty weeks (nearly four months), Pauline hadn't made the top-twenty news stories. She and the party were a dead duck. The 'I've been murdered' story went everywhere and kept going in different versions for several weeks. Pauline Hanson's One Nation was back at the top of the news – not only in general news, TV, radio, newspapers and magazines, but people were even writing comedy skits about it and the 'If you're seeing me now, I've been murdered' concept was even turned into a comedy-driven advertising campaign for roasted chicken.

Within a week or so of the program airing, the next poll showed support for One Nation had doubled, and it just kept climbing through into the new year and on to the Queensland state election, where the party received 23 per cent of the vote, outpolling the Liberals and the National Party.

Call it a stunt, call it whatever you like, it's results that count and the story of the threat facing Pauline and my way of exposing it relaunched Pauline Hanson's One Nation. At a meeting following the release of the 'I've been murdered' clip, Labor identity Bob Ellis told me I was 'an evil genius'.

I'd worked on numerous election campaigns for all levels of government, local, state and federal, but the only time I'd been entirely in charge of a campaign were the times I successfully ran local government campaigns for myself and others.

The Queensland state election presented me with the opportunity to control essentially everything, state wide. It's safe to say no single person had ever done that before – I personally created and or oversaw every facet of the campaign. One Nation co-founder David Ettridge also acknowledged that I was 'the only person the party had with the experience and skills to strategise preference flows, train candidates and coordinate their material needs ...'

This situation came about for two reasons: firstly, as the party's principal adviser and founder, I had a lot of pull; but perhaps even more than that, One Nation was such a hodgepodge of political newcomers, that no-one knew enough to question me all that much. And in that sense, there was the simple fact that, as well-meaning as so many One Nation members were, they just didn't have the knowledge and experience to run election campaigns, so much of it fell naturally to me.

To begin with I had to train the candidates, about eighty across Queensland. I held three weekend-long seminars in different locations to which the candidates and key members of their campaign teams travelled. Taking people, who for the most part, had no understanding of politics or campaigning at all, and imparting all that was necessary for them to be proficient, in one weekend, was no easy task. Amongst so many things, I taught them presentation and recorded their efforts, so they could see themselves in action and be corrected as appropriate. I trained them in knocking on doors and communication in general because, of course, politics is all about communication.

I personally designed the how-to-vote cards, posters and other related materials. I oversaw policy development, briefed the candidates responsible for policy announcements and attended their press conferences to control the media on their behalf. Statewide-related press announcements, such as how we would distribute preferences, were made by me, and I coordinated Pauline Hanson's movements to areas where I knew her visits would serve the greatest benefit.

I did whatever I needed to get it all done. I had lots of energy and I expended it 24/7. I had no choice – these were not tasks I could delegate, I had to do it myself.

If I was ever acknowledged for my across-the-board role in that election, any such appreciation of what I did has been lost, and, or, deliberately obliterated over time. It wouldn't suit those in control of One Nation today to remember what I did at the beginning.

The National Party (now LNP) were desperate for One Nation preferences, so I came to an arrangement that gave me access to their polling, a luxury for which we didn't have any money. This allowed me to determine where our best chances were across Queensland. I was the only person with access to this polling, so no-one else was aware of who I was positioning, or why.

In terms of funds, the party didn't have any money at all, so we came up with an arrangement where candidates would fundraise and pay their own costs, and when the electoral office refunded the party based on the number of votes following the election, we would refund the candidates 80 per cent of the funds received from the electoral commission. That worked well. We managed to run an election campaign without any money, and the result would mean candidates got a good portion back while the party would get 20 per cent of funds received to aid ongoing activities. As a matter of interest, the major political parties do not refund candidates or individual campaigns, but keep all proceeds received from the electoral commission.

The polling I had access to, courtesy of the National Party, made it clear to me there was a chance for One Nation to win the balance of power and that neither the Coalition nor Labor would be able to form government without support from One Nation MPs. To do this, I had to bolster certain National and Liberal Party seats by making sure One Nation preferences were directed their way. This was crucial in seats One Nation could not win but where One Nation preferences would decide the outcome.

I was successful in making this happen in all but two seats – those One Nation candidates refused absolutely to direct their preferences to any person or party. Nothing I could do would change their minds. I even had Pauline speak to them, but they held out against her, so we were stuck with these two critical areas where our preferences would not be directed on our how-to-votes.

As I'd predicted, those two seats fell to Labor. Each of the sitting Liberal MPs lost by less than 100 votes, while more than 5000 One Nation preferences in each seat, that should have been sent to them, remained unallocated.

Both candidates contacted me after the election and apologised, because they now understood why I was so adamant about their preferences needing to go to the Liberal Party because it was in One Nation's interests. It was after the fact and useless, but at least they could now see what I told them was going to happen, did in fact turn out exactly as I'd explained.

The election was an outstanding success, and without doubt my greatest ever campaigning success. Though few know it, those two seats would have given One Nation the balance of power and the Coalition would have been forced to negotiate with us to be able to remain in government.

Pauline Hanson's One Nation won eleven seats at its first ever election. We outpolled the National Party and the Liberal Party and now had more MPs in the Queensland state parliament than the Liberal Party. It was utterly amazing, extraordinary in every sense – no political party up until then, other than Labor and the Coalition, had ever won a lower house seat in any parliament in Australia. We'd made history!

Hilariously though, and upsetting to say the least, some in One Nation were disappointed with the result. They expected to actually win the overall election and have a One Nation premier. I was often beset by people with absolutely no idea.

Within a matter of months, it all went to hell as the MPs got ahead of themselves, conveniently forgetting how they were elected and through what means – PHON. Self-importance set in and got the better of them. I could design a campaign to get them elected, but I wasn't able to keep their political ignorance and egos in check. One thing led to another and they failed to understand they were little to nothing without the party. They broke away, most forming their own party, and all but one of them were wiped from the face of the earth at the next election.

The outcome of the 1998 Queensland election gave forces within the Liberal Party the ammunition they needed to make sure One Nation wouldn't get Coalition preferences at the coming federal election. It was spun that One Nation had been responsible for the defeat of the Liberal/National coalition and this had occurred because of preference deals. It was an easy tale to spin given most people don't understand such things and there wasn't anyone in Coalition circles willing to rebut this nonsense.

The fact was, of the eleven seats One Nation had won, five were taken from the Coalition and six from Labor – the Coalition had lost the election themselves. One Nation became a handy scapegoat for those wanting a convenient excuse to mask their own incompetence.

I knew the federal election would be soon. Technically, it didn't have to be until 1999, but most expected it towards the end of 1998, so with the Queensland state election behind us, there wasn't much time to prepare for the even bigger challenge of the federal election.

Sadly, Pauline Hanson was among those who failed to understand how we'd done so well in Queensland, and I suppose that shouldn't come as very much of a surprise. Pauline, helped by those always whispering in her ear, had come to believe herself to be the Messiah. She was happy to see herself portrayed as Joan of Arc – someone actually painted a portrait depicting her as Saint Joan. Perhaps Pauline had forgotten Joan was burnt at the stake, or perhaps she never knew?

In August of 1998, it became apparent I'd lost control of Pauline – she was so wrapped up in her own greatness, infallibility and the public's adulation, that there was no making her see sense. She had made that mistake so many make – she believed her own press. She believed she was unbeatable; she believed she was the Messiah!

The party was doing amazingly in the polls; we really had the major parties scared. And then Pauline released the 2 per cent Easy Tax. Pauline and all around her thought it was the stuff of genius. Imagine, a system that worked in such a way that no-one would ever pay more than 2 per cent tax.

Yes, everyone around Pauline was on side, except me – I was the only person opposed to the Easy Tax. I first tried explaining it was a GST multiplying on every transaction and we were opposing the GST the Howard government planned to introduce, so how could we have a GST of our own? When that failed, I pointed out that even if it worked, it was being sold as if it was just a 2 per cent tax – no-one would believe a 2 per cent tax was possible. As much as everyone would love to only pay 2 per cent tax, it's not believable and it doesn't matter how good something is if people don't believe it.

Nothing I said made a difference. Pauline was no longer listening to me and didn't understand the mechanics of the tax herself anyway. I couldn't stop it – I was alone in opposition to this nonsense.

Then I was forced to arrange a press conference where Pauline was going to launch this mathematical nightmare of which she had no actual understanding. I didn't want to be in the room, but there I was standing up the back hoping and praying that somehow the Easy Tax would just disappear. Within five minutes, the media were tying Pauline in knots and I started to hope and pray I would somehow disappear!

It was a huge story – the Easy Tax was everywhere. It was rubbish, it was easily discredited and as I'd tried to explain, just plain damn unbelievable, and Pauline on camera, showing she didn't have a clue how it worked, was the last straw.

Our support dropped about 30 per cent virtually overnight. That was the immediate feedback from our better candidates, and the next poll in several seats confirmed the losses the Easy Tax had caused. From there forwards, I knew we were done. I had to salvage what I could, but Pauline dug her heels in, wasn't listening, wouldn't believe the polling or the feedback and was still trying to pitch the Easy Tax.

For me at that stage, the one win that was still possible was Pauline herself – she could still win her seat and at least we could rebuild from there. Well, that's what I told myself. Once again, however, Pauline was the fly in the ointment – she didn't think she needed to campaign. I couldn't get her to knock on a single door and despite having loads of cash donated for her personal re-election campaign, she wouldn't spend it. Pauline would be the only candidate in history who was penny pinching on spending the donations she'd received because she was trying to not only get elected, but make a profit at the same time. She wouldn't let me do any direct mail or initiate any campaign strategies I had for her re-election, because she didn't want to spend any money. I'm not aware of other candidates keeping monies donated to their election campaigns. Usually, candidates don't come into contact with such funds, but Pauline had people handing her cash in envelopes.

I spent the last weeks of the campaign travelling with her trying to salvage what I could, but unlike the Queensland state election, I didn't have the authority to make things happen or stop stupidity. We didn't have preferences from anyone and we were being choked at the end of a rope. Pauline remained absolutely confident she would be re-elected, right up until the moment she conclusively lost.

No amount of what you know, and understand can be done, amounts to a can of beans if you can't get people doing it. This wasn't the first time I'd be forced to watch on helplessly while everything around me burst into flames.

Even though One Nation received nearly a million votes in the lower house and over a million in the Senate, all we had was one person elected. In terms of votes, it was an amazing result; in terms of seats, it was a shocker.

Two things destroyed Pauline Hanson's One Nation in the 1998 federal election – one was the 2 per cent Easy Tax, the other was Pauline Hanson. We couldn't have done better without her, but ultimately, she stopped us from doing better with her.

I'd been the candidate for the Senate for New South Wales in 1998 and I secured 9.6 per cent of the vote. Under any normal circumstances, that would have been enough, but we were deprived of preferences and after Pauline adopted the 2 per cent Easy Tax, any chance to win just slipped away. Such are the results when relying so much on one person. I'd meant to build a political party that would give Australians a genuine alternative to what was already on offer, but been beaten from within.

New South Wales has a four-year election cycle with polling day always falling on a Saturday in March. That meant with this October federal election now behind us, I had five months to prepare a very depressed party for another huge effort. Pauline was still a blubbering, inconsolable mess pointing the finger of blame everywhere other than where it should have been pointing – at her.

Back in Sydney, I was mostly free to organise the New South Wales election without too much interference. Following the party preselecting me for the number-one spot on the ticket for the upper house (Legislative Council), I once again set off to train candidates, create the how-to-votes and all other election materials. That was a simpler job this time around as I was able to use the same basic formats I'd used successfully in Queensland.

The other thing that was helpful was that unlike the Queensland state election, the party now had money. Nearly 2.9 million dollars had come through the electoral funding secured by all the votes for One Nation in the federal election. Most had to be returned to federal candidates, but there was still more than enough left over for the New South Wales campaign.

After the New South Wales election, there was a carry-on by the knockers about the million dollars spent to get David Oldfield elected, but what they conveniently neglected to mention was we were due to receive more in funding, because of the votes cast in New South Wales, than we'd spent on the actual campaign.

As you'd have noted from above, I was elected to the New South Wales Parliament, and with more than a quota. Had the person in charge of lodging our preference documents turned up on time to do it, we would likely have had a second person elected to the upper house with me.

We were relatively successful in New South Wales – the support wasn't anything like Queensland and there'd been a lot of heart lost after getting so many votes in the federal election yet only finishing with one senator, but now, once again, there was hope. And that is how I saw my election – as a way of fighting back. I had an eight-year term ahead of me and reasonable resources to rebuild the party while making myself heard on issues the others wouldn't raise. It wasn't the platform provided by the federal parliament, but it would have to do. At least I was now able to deliver my own speeches rather than listening to Pauline waffle and um and ah through what I'd written for her.

It would be an understatement to say Pauline was less than helpful in the New South Wales campaign. She was on the One Nation payroll at the time, but a cattle prod was needed to get her to do anything. When she arrived in Sydney for election night, I met her and took her to her hotel. Less than fifteen minutes after I left her, as I was crossing the Harbour Bridge, David Ettridge called to tell me she was organising to jump a cab back to the airport and leave. It appeared that the hotel wasn't good enough – it was only four and a half stars, not five and we hadn't left her a bottle of wine. Apparently Pauline hadn't heard of picking up the phone and dialling room service? Pauline appeared to be bored and terribly put out that no-one was entertaining her and the prospect of spending an hour or two at the hotel on her own prior to heading off to the tally room was more than she could stand.

As it was, when we ultimately got to the tally room to watch the results unfold, that was more than she could stand too – a night that wasn't 100 per cent about her was too much for Pauline. Rather than watch the results unfold across the state, the salaried president of the party got David Ettridge to take her away from the tally room to a Bee Gees concert.

With the New South Wales election behind us, one of the silliest things that happened early and got Pauline's nose further out of joint was her attendance at my maiden speech. Pauline's nose was already well and truly out of joint just by virtue of me being in parliament and her not being in parliament.

The party always catered for her. Immediately after she lost her seat in 1998, she went straight onto the party payroll, but a few appearances was all that was expected of her – she was paid for being Pauline Hanson.

On the night of my maiden speech, I discussed with her where she would sit. There was limited space behind where I would be speaking, but I pointed out it was better for her to sit in the public gallery, with the hundreds of One Nation members also in attendance. It made sense that the self-appointed 'mother of the nation', would sit in the middle of her own party members, who had filled the gallery to overflowing.

Someone got her going that she should be sitting with my family behind me, and before you know it, where she was sitting was taken as some kind of snub by me. I didn't find this out until months later. Imagine that, the beloved Pauline Hanson, always touted as just an ordinary Australian, 'a woman of the people', showed she was too good to sit with her own fan club!

In the second half of 2000, David Ettridge decided to create political parties as a way of feeding preferences to One Nation and, as a member of parliament, I was able to help him. It wasn't a new idea; it had been done quite a bit and was very effective. If every other political party was going to continue to collude and put One Nation last, then it made sense to try and create some preference feeds of our own.

However, Pauline jumped on this as a way of getting me out of the party. She accused me of disloyalty and a range of other things, despite it being clear I was facilitating acts in One Nation's interest. There were a couple of showdowns, but logic and sense could never stand in the way of Pauline and an angry mob who'd believe the moon was made of green cheese if she told them it was true.

And so it came to pass that Pauline Hanson expelled me from One Nation, via a press release. The person who came up with the idea for the party, was responsible for the ideology of the party and who wrote the speech which launched the party, as well as the twenty-four founding platforms and principles, was 'fired'.

Pauline didn't have the power to do that, but she has never been one to let rules or a constitution or any other bothersome technicalities get in her way. As I write, I can hear her screaming, 'I'm Pauline Hanson!' Whenever she yelled like that, I wondered whether she was telling us or reminding herself.

Despite the law being on my side in the matter, I knew there was no point resisting – the time to coexist with Pauline Hanson had passed. Besides, I had nearly seven years to go in parliament and I was the registered officer of One Nation in New South Wales. Apparently, she hadn't thought that through, and she moved to have the party deregistered in New South Wales and the electoral commissioner was informed that I'd registered the party fraudulently.

How does the party's founder and its only parliamentary member register the party fraudulently? And on that, isn't it just a little too convenient that the notion of fraud regarding the registration only became an issue after I was 'expelled'? Why wasn't there a problem with the party's registration and my alleged 'fraud' before I was unconstitutionally removed as a member?

Excuse my approach to these absurd allegations: clearly there was no problem and no fraud. It was an ill-considered ruse to get the party deregistered so I would no longer be the registered officer. So, because of the infighting within One Nation and the accusations of wrongful registration, the electoral commissioner chose to deregister the party and in doing that removed the obligation to pay nearly $400,000 in funding to the New South Wales party over the following three years.

Continuing on the theme of Pauline not thinking ahead, she didn't see the loss of $400,000 coming, but what she also didn't see was that as the last registered officer of the party, I was the only person who could authorise the re-registration.

The party was split, especially in New South Wales. About half the members remained with me, so we relatively easily put together the support of the 750 members required to re-register the party, and One Nation New South Wales was born.

My work now entailed the same things as other members of the upper house, we reviewed legislation and, where appropriate, attempted to amend matters or speak on behalf of the amendments of others. Unless you're into the supposed 'power' of being a member of parliament, it's pretty boring and unbelievably frustrating. It's an office job with the pretence of being of consequence.

Perhaps that's a little unfair, it is an important job and there are actually some fine people doing it, but there were also a lot who were grubs filled with self-importance and snobbery, with no genuine regard for the people they purported to represent.

Then, of course, there were those who were only there to steal whatever they could and used their positions to line their own pockets. Numerous pollies I knew while in parliament were ultimately caught for corruption and forced out of parliament – some were jailed. The most infamous of these is probably Eddie Obeid. Eventually he was found guilty and went to jail. I always thought Eddie to be shady beyond belief, but I couldn't have imagined the multimillion-dollar deals he was doing to benefit himself and his extended family.

Parliament is entirely party-line based, so in many respects there is no point to making speeches or taking part in what is ridiculously referred to as 'debate'. The outcomes are always known before the 'debates' begin. It's all done in behind-closed-door negotiations.

Call me silly, but I hated, and indeed still do hate, that no amount of facts or rational debate are going to change anyone's vote. The whole process verges on fraud. It's disappointing to say the least; more like soul destroying. The only real point to the debates is for the purposes of record keeping, and almost the only reason to speak in the debate is to be seen to be representing your constituency and having it on record to demonstrate that's what you've done.

My uncle Ted (Edward) Peate Oldfield, was a state member in Western Australia for fifteen years and prior to that, on the equivalent of a town council. He was a helluva drunk and it ultimately killed him, but he was a fair dinkum bloke, an infantry combat veteran of WW II, and he deeply cared about the people he represented.

When my dad was approached by the Liberal Party to stand for parliament, Ted, who was his younger brother, advised him against it. He told Dad it was the dirtiest, most rotten business a person could be in and Dad would be best staying out of it. Dad took his little brother's advice.

If it was so rotten and awful in Ted's day in the 1950s and 1960s, you can only imagine how much worse it is today. I understood my role and what was required of me and worked at that accordingly, but I considered my primary function to be speaking out loudly on the things that must be said and were never said because of political correctness.

I was still hopeful One Nation could be rebuilt, but given the split and the appalling bad luck we'd had with the nature of Pauline and some other elected members, it was an impossible task. There were some good people elected through One Nation, though there were others who were nothing types, and being a parliamentarian had granted them success and recognition well beyond anything their abilities might have ever brought them.

I'm firmly of the view you should never make something of someone who has never made anything of themselves. Politics can do that, it sometimes takes people who shouldn't be near sensible conversation, let alone public debate, and suddenly makes them of consequence in the scheme of things, when really, they're not.

The major parties are looking for plausibly sellable candidates, they're not looking for the proverbial rocket scientist. Yes, they need stand-outs, but a lot of MPs just have to be relatively acceptable to their electorate and know which side of the parliament to sit on when a vote is called. And that's not hard given there is a party whip (MP who acts as a coordinator) to direct them, and as a general rule of thumb, if you're sitting with people who aren't in your party, it's most likely you're on the wrong side of the room!

The party isn't all that interested in the ideas of individuals. It tends to have its own agenda and simply needs bums on seats to carry that agenda out. Sad as that is, it's hard to see how it could be different, because when it's all said and done, the system relies on people to feed it and make it run, and people are so hellishly damaged and so easily corrupted, and those they fear the most are those who aren't like them.

I had eight years in the New South Wales upper house (Legislative Council) and I think I did as much as I could under very difficult circumstances where honesty and a wish to fix things are character flaws.

Even as I write this now, it depresses me. Some people deserve a lot better than what the administration of our lives coughs up – some people, not all. It was always terribly hard to see people who truly had a right to a better outcome, but just know it wasn't going to happen for them.

There are wins. It isn't all bad and there are good people in politics; though, the dirtier it gets, the dirtier and more mistrustful the good people get in their bid to combat the evil among us.

I was without the protection and support of an established party structure, so I recognise I'm perhaps more jaded than most, but what I more so recognise, is despite what I know, what I've seen and how little faith I have in people, I can't help but hope for better. When you feel like that, the cold hard light of day doesn't take you by surprise, it just disappoints you so much more than it should. Even now, I suffer from wanting there to be good guys and bad guys and for the distinction between the two groups to be clear.

I managed to raise my own legislation and get it passed into law – almost something of an impossibility when not in government. I started out thinking it was a reasonably straightforward matter, but as soon as competing interests unconcerned about the issue itself get involved, nothing is simple.

The legal drinking age is eighteen and there were various laws in place to stop anyone under eighteen from drinking alcohol, but smoking, well that's a strangely different matter. The only thing preventing someone from smoking was laws making it illegal to sell cigarettes to or procure cigarettes for anyone under eighteen years of age. It wasn't illegal as such to smoke if under eighteen, or certainly not in any way that was able to be enforced. Sorry if you are a smoker, but you know the old line, every cigarette is doing you damage. It didn't make sense to me that there wasn't more action able to be undertaken on underage smoking.

Realistically, smoking is far more dangerous to your health than drinking, unless you become an alcoholic, in which case perhaps they're more on a par. Or at least, let me suggest that a couple of drinks here and there aren't doing much if any harm and certain alcoholic drinks likely have some health benefits. Whereas cigarettes – inhaling death with every breath!

My plan was to introduce legislation for underage smoking that mirrored underage drinking. This would mean if police found kids smoking, they could require them to produce identification and if they were underage then the police could confiscate the cigarettes as they would with alcohol. Further, if they found the kids had produced fake IDs, they were able to confiscate those as well.

To me, that all seemed pretty straightforward – simply apply underage smoking laws in exactly the same way underage drinking laws were already applied. Quite often, when police would happen upon underage drinkers, they would be smoking as well – it would seem the laws would go well together. One of the things I found out early in my quest to try to further remove cigarettes from kids, is some lawmakers aren't concerned about the effects of alcohol, except in the case where someone's drinking endangers others. So they weren't all that concerned about kids smoking because no matter how much they smoked, they weren't by virtue of that deemed any danger to anyone else.

I found the Greens were unwilling to support my bill because they said it would be just another way for the police to come down on young people. Typical anti-establishment position of the Greens in that they see the police as part of the problem rather than being helpful.

The Labor Party were worried they'd anger seventeen-year-olds, who would then soon be voting and not had time to forget Labor were complicit in confiscating their smokes – yes, I'm serious, that was their main objection.

The coalition spokesperson for this area was a left-wing Liberal

Party MP and hellishly angry that One Nation existed, so anything raised by me wasn't even going to get a hearing, let alone support.

As a One Nation MLC and later an independent, I was grouped into what was referred to as the crossbench, such being that we were neither the government nor the Opposition.

In my time the crossbench was quite a block, getting as high as thirteen members out of a total of forty-two MLCs in the upper house. Neither the government nor the Opposition had the numbers to do anything without most of the crossbench on side, so there was a little bit of room for negotiating, but as there was only one of me, the numbers were near impossible to muster.

Perhaps one of the most distressing aspects of passing legislation is that support isn't necessarily forthcoming because the matter is seen as important, but, rather, because it is seen as unimportant. If an issue was unimportant to a member, that was your best chance to get their support on the basis that they would want yours in return somewhere down the line for something that was important to them.

After nearly three years of negotiation – yes, nearly three years – I managed to get the Labor government to support my bill and I persuaded enough of the crossbench to vote with me, and hence my legislation was successful. The Greens and Coalition members voted in a block against police being able to confiscate cigarettes from children – how proud of themselves they must have been.

The trick to issues like this is hardly anyone in the public will ever know it happened and certainly won't have any idea how anyone voted. Picture a supposedly sensible member of parliament being confronted by an articulate, informed voter and asked to justify why they voted to stop police from being able to take cigarettes off ten-year-olds, or, indeed, anyone under eighteen.

With further fracturing of One Nation and Pauline Hanson splitting the vote at the 2003 election by running for the upper house as an independent, it became evident I was trying to keep something alive that had already died.

I'll note here that Pauline decided she'd run for parliament pretty much anywhere – it was an embarrassing time where she seemed to have the attitude that if there was an election, she was going to be in it; supposedly a Queenslander through and through, but gee, she thought the New South Wales upper house looked nice.

I couldn't do that. I have very strong views on representation. I'm one of those crazy people who thinks you should play sport for the suburb, or city or state in which you reside. I would never have moved from my local area just to get into parliament. That seemed like a very wrong thing to me, an ingenuous act. I suppose it's the nationalist in me, on a micro level. The insincerity so clearly attached to opportunistically moving is a bridge too far for me. Maybe I'm on my own in that?

Not long after the 2003 election, I was approached by a shadow minister (Opposition spokesperson) from the Coalition, who was sussing me out about returning to the Liberal Party – some in their ranks appreciated me. After a meeting or two, as I pondered what had only recently seemed impossible, it became evident there were a few Liberal parliamentarians in on this plan.

There wasn't anything more I could do with One Nation, the party I'd founded; perhaps there was something I could do from within the Liberal Party. After all, my original plan was to change the Liberal Party and, to a degree, I'd done that.

I went to the president of One Nation New South Wales and explained the situation. He was a wise and eminently decent man who on many occasions had shown himself to genuinely care for Australia. His name was Ian Hale and I liked him very much.

Ian told me, if it could be done, I should leave One Nation New South Wales and join the Liberal Party. He was firmly of the view that if I was to make a difference, then my best chance to do that was by joining the Libs who wanted me, and then accomplish what I could from inside the party.

I went back to the Liberals to tell them I was willing to rejoin the Liberal Party. I knew by this time there were three shadow ministers and a couple of other MPs who were involved. Their next step was to get a person of influence from outside the party to tell the Liberal Opposition leader that David Oldfield retuning to the Liberal Party was a good idea. They had just the person in mind for the job and funnily enough, it was a person I knew well, so it was me who made the approach.

The very eminent citizen I met with had a great deal of influence with the Liberal Party and clearly, in particular, with John Brogden, the state Opposition leader. That person of influence just picked up the phone and told John Brogden that he should accept me into the parliamentary party.

Within a few days, I had a meeting with John Brogden and he agreed in principle that it could be done, but we'd need to position me over a period rather than just being One Nation one day and a Liberal the next. I thought that to be a fair and understandable approach. Frankly, the idea I was actually returning to the Liberals seemed a bit far-fetched to me, yet here I was, in the office of the Opposition leader discussing the timetable for that to happen.

There were a number of meetings with John Brogden and other Liberals over a few months and then John set a date for the press conference we would hold jointly to announce my return. However, as this was happening, others in the Liberal Party, concerned as to the threat/competition I posed to them, were simultaneously working to derail the plan.

John Brogden himself wasn't an entirely willing participant and, indeed, it's possible he was employing stalling tactics looking for a way out. Ultimately, there was enough pressure from behind the scenes to put the plan on ice. If there was ever a chance of pulling it off, it was lost when Brogden had to resign from parliament.

Returning to the Liberals – how odd that would have been, for them and for me; still, it was nice quite a few of them wanted me back. Just knowing that in itself was worth the experience.

I still had a couple of years to run on my current term, and I proceeded as an independent, doing the job as expected and fulfilling my obligations as a parliamentarian, but it wasn't what I wanted. I require purpose in my life; the notion of being in parliament as just a job, as a way to make a living as a glorified bureaucrat, just wasn't in me, so in late 2005, I decided not to stand for re-election in 2007, and I announced that publicly in June 2006.

There were some options open to me for re-election, but I would have been doing it just to stay there and I'd never viewed being a politician as a lifelong career. For me it was more about fighting a war and when the war is won or lost, it's time to go home. I'd known since being elected in 1999 that I was fighting a losing battle, but of course you cannot win by giving up, so sometimes you fight the losing battle till there is a chance to breakout and change the course of the fight. But the breakout never came.

I hadn't surrendered; however, I no longer had a field over which to fight. My time to go home had come, so I quietly retired at the 2007 election, with a plan to go into the media.

> Well, the poll has brought your rather unusual political career to an end, and I have to say your good humour, charm and reasonable attitude to most questions have made your time in politics far more productive and less difficult than the pundits predicted. I hope your future offers equally robust opportunities for the use of your talents.
>
> – The Honourable Morris Iemma MP, Premier of New South Wales, from a letter written 2 May 2007, following my retirement from parliament in March 2007

Ah, but should the story of my personal time in politics just end with a lovely farewell letter from Morris or should I note the sexual harassment and swinging? Well I understand salacious details are interesting to quite a lot of people, and it's fair to say there are more than a few of those stories that relate to me. I'm not planning to join the #MeToo movement any time soon and, let's face it, those involved don't tend to subscribe to the preposterous suggestion men could ever be victims of such crimes; but I was, more than once, and the perpetrators were various people of both sexes.

As a naive bloke in my early days with the Liberal party, I was jumped in a car by a party official. There I was, parked outside the party headquarters simply chatting and giving off no signals whatsoever when the married woman beside me suddenly leapt on top of me yelling, 'Take me David'! A person who I thought of as a friend, supporter, and in many respects, a mentor, was now finding herself being held off by me as I quickly tried to explain she had misunderstood our association. I nicely explained I wasn't interested, and this was wrong on many levels, not the least of which was that she was married.

It truly was very disturbing at the time, but I took it well and I was mostly concerned that my knocking this dear lady back was hurtful to her, and whether she would ever be helpful again. However, looking back on it with 2019 eyes, it was a gross violation of my rights and more than crossed a line of trust and I genuinely didn't see it coming. All the time I thought this person was interested in me because of my political potential when perhaps all along all she wanted was to screw me. Gee, I wonder how many women have felt just as used and abused as I have described?

Then there was the minister's chief of staff. This time a youngish intelligent chap, who silly me hadn't even noted was gay, not that it would have mattered. At the end of a boozy party in the minister's office, without any warning I saw, he shoved his hand down the front of my pants; in his defence, perhaps he was merely looking for some nuts to nibble on while enjoying his wine, but I digress.

Again, I had that embarrassment of having to strongly withdraw his hand and leap backwards, while simultaneously explaining I wasn't gay and while I was 'almost' flattered, it wasn't going to happen. He didn't give up there and it took quite a bit of calm but clear talk by me for him to finally get the message. Again I was left wondering what impact my refusing this advance (sexual assault), from a person of political significance and position, might have on the plans for my career. I wonder about all the females who have had exactly those thoughts, but again, such worries aren't generally considered associated with males, and anyway clearly it was all my fault for ending up alone in his company with us both intoxicated, oh wait …

Then there was the lawyer in the taxi and the female senator, not from the party you might think, and on both of those occasions, I was also left rocked by what my rejection of these very forward people would do to my future.

Looking back on just those incidents I have noted here, it was terrible that I or anyone would be subjected to such situations, especially so when there is the matter of career, and the people involved being able to either help or hurt you, depending on how they felt after being knocked back.

Did I feel dirty or psychologically damaged by any of these experiences? No. At the time I just took it in my stride, used that tired old line about the problem wasn't them, but in fact me, and did all I could to stay friendly in the hope my unwillingness to get physical wouldn't be held against me when it mattered.

After becoming a parliamentarian myself, there was a widespread story that Lisa (my wife) and I are or were swingers, which has dogged us for years, and even to this day I bump into people who know the story, because they know someone who knows someone who knows all about it.

It came up in context of me writing this book as those reading the initial drafts asked me why I'd left out that I am a swinger. Prior to that, I genuinely thought no-one had ever really taken that story seriously – I soon found out I was wrong, wrong, wrong!

I've long been of the view that what happens sexually between people is not a matter for public discussion, but the willingness of others to gossip, often in complete ignorance of any facts, continues to amaze me. There I am, naive still!

As I've said before, lies have a life of their own and people love a good tale, but there is nothing at all appealing to me about watching Lisa have sex with someone else or engaging with her in some kind of group action – I'm sure she feels the same.

I can trace this rumour back to its roots. It started when a gossip column printed a story about us having a couple of champagne breakfasts with a particular media couple, with whom we were good friends, alongside a nice paparazzi photo of the four of us. Given public photographs of those friends, and what was apparently understood about their lifestyle, it was immediately determined we must also be swingers, and indeed, must have spent the previous couple of nights with them, swinging!

Lisa and I were essentially guilty by association it would seem. But sorry to disappoint, we have never been swingers. The whole story was a complete fabrication that has grown out of all proportion and all without so much as a skerrick of truth.

I know what you're thinking: if he denies it, then it must be true. So, considering guilt by association, I'll put it this way, I once bumped into Roger Rogerson and he kindly bought me a beer, but I haven't killed anyone; well, not yet anyway!

Some think politics to be very, sex and drugs and rock and roll, but I mostly avoided the sex and never did the drugs, and though I admit to often enjoying the rock and roll, politicians are fooling themselves if they think they're cool.

I found my time in politics to be enormously unsettling and disappointing, but it would be awfully dishonest not to acknowledge there were lots of laughs and quite a bit of fun along the way.

Leaving Tony

David has remarkable powers of concentration and great single-mindedness. He never left anything to chance.

– The Hon. Tony Abbott MP,
May 1997

The Hon. Tony Abbott MP is the former federal member for Warringah and a former Prime Minister of Australia. When he was a parliamentary secretary in the government of The Hon. John Howard MP, I was his private secretary. One of the more difficult decisions I've had to make was leaving Tony Abbott.

Clearly, it was towards the end of my time with Tony that I created the political party, Pauline Hanson's One Nation, and so a long battle began. There have been many stories about that time, but never any accurate reports on the events that led up to that decision and how I ultimately came to leave Tony's office on a Friday and turn up, out of the blue, as Pauline Hanson's advisor on the following Monday. You are about to read the first real account of what and how all this came about, written by the only person who knows why and how it happened – me.

It is extraordinary how people with little if any involvement in what I am about to write, portrayed themselves as experts on my thoughts and motives for leaving Tony Abbott and forming One Nation. I liked Tony and I liked working for him. He relied on me and I did a good job for him. Yes, there was the small matter of being treacherous and disloyal and jumping ship to create Pauline Hanson's One Nation, but that's just the enemy's view; when considered in context, that isn't what happened at all.

Here's what was in my mind and how it all unfolded.

In the first instance, re accusations of treachery and disloyalty, neither Tony nor the Liberal Party owned me. I was a paid-up member of the Liberal Party, indeed, a patron-level member, which meant I paid much more than a standard member. I got nothing else in return – the hundreds of dollars extra I paid for membership were effectively an annual donation. The point being, I paid the Liberal Party, they didn't pay me, and my loyalty, if that is even the right word, was contingent on my belief the Liberal Party were doing the right thing.

I determined the Liberal Party was not pursuing what I believed was in Australia's interest, so I decided to do something about that. I didn't defect or change sides as such, I actually came up with an entirely new party from scratch. I was completely within my rights to do that. I repeat, I wasn't owned by the Liberal Party.

Then there is the matter of working for Tony. For at least some people, this will likely seem a greyer area, and I understand that, but with context and perspective, any reasonable person would accept why I did what I did.

The first thing to understand is that politics isn't a clean game where everyone is a good sport and there is a set of rules by which all the ladies and gentlemen play with honesty and openness. Maybe you already get that? The opposite is the case. Whilst I believed, and still do believe it is necessary to be politically open and honest with the public, this is impossible in the dirty, behind-the-scenes game that always lives in the shadows of the ugliness that is politics.

I decided there was a way to try and do what I thought was best for Australia. It was a big ask, to take on the long-established political system of the two major parties.

I couldn't just announce what I was doing. Politics is like a war – you can't give the enemy a heads-up on what you're planning, and the bottom line is that once I chose the path I did, all parties of any note became the enemy. The Coalition, Labor, the Greens, Democrats, they would all be against me – and they were!

After I met Pauline Hanson, my initial thoughts related to utilising what was happening around Pauline to push the Liberals in the right direction. I didn't meet her and immediately decide to form another political party. In the first instance, I thought she could be the catalyst to addressing much of what was missing from the party of which I was a member, the Liberal Party. I talked to Tony about using her to push things in the direction I believed necessary, especially against multiculturalism, immigration and globalism. Tony said no and told me to, 'stay away from her'.

Below is an account of my position from a feature in *The Australian* newspaper on 28 August 2003 entitled 'The Oldfield Agenda', by Megan Saunders:

> But in a surprising twist, he maintains that it wasn't until his last couple of months in Abbott's office – then parliamentary secretary to education minister Amanda Vanstone – that he made up his mind to leave.
>
> His grand plan until that point was to use Hanson's influence to shift the Coalition further to the right. The decision to leave came after he spoke to Abbott.
>
> 'It was made pretty clear to me that there was no way of moving the Liberal Party on the basis of anything Hanson was doing, so I left it at that, but disagreed in silence and decided that the only thing I could do to move Australia more towards the Right ... was to join Hanson, help her form a party and support that movement.'

In the areas that really concerned me, it was evident the new Howard government was not going to do anything. They had to be pushed and I decided I'd found the way to do the pushing.

Now the next part is going to seem really unusual, but hey that's me, and you're reading this to get an understanding of why I did what I did, instead of the ill-informed speculation of commentators who have still never spoken to me about the reasons things unfolded as they did. Rather than being disloyal to Tony, I was very loyal to him and very cognisant of how much he relied on me. Don't misunderstand me, Tony has extraordinary abilities and I wasn't indispensable, but I was doing work for him that I couldn't just drop – at least I thought so at the time.

Tony was the parliamentary secretary for DEETYA – which stood for Department of Education, Employment Training and Youth Affairs. I took my job very seriously and Tony knew and appreciated that. My title was private secretary, but that was a bit silly and came about because apparently only one person in the office was allowed to have the title, advisor. However, the person in that role's advice was restricted to inter-factional information and local branch plotting. The actual portfolio advice was constructed solely by me, and I worked with a departmental liaison officer who was excellent, utterly diligent and the very best of her profession.

Tony's direct portfolio responsibilities were Austudy (student education) Abstudy (Aboriginal student education) and ICS (Isolated Children's Scheme), and the liaison and reporting of matters therein was attended to by me. I regularly dealt with the drafting of media releases and departmental correspondence. I even had an occasional involvement with CES (Commonwealth Employment Services) offices and at one time helped select which of those offices at different locations around Australia would be closed.

I guess most people think the offices of parliamentarians are staffed by the quickest brightest minds hired for their abilities? Well maybe you didn't think that was the case, and to a considerable degree, it isn't the case. It doesn't matter to which party a parliamentarian belongs, there's more chance than not that their office has at least a few staff members who aren't there because of their talent. One might be a local party hack who keeps an eye on the local party branches, another might be someone from the party to whom a substantial favour is owed or the relative of a party powerbroker. Depending on the demographic of the electorate, there'll perhaps also be someone with seemingly close ties, or some tie to the community. In the worst cases, the person might have the job primarily because of their ethnicity.

Then there's the personally ambitious character that the MP wants to keep close so as to try to control that person's ambition, or, as seen recently with the Barnaby Joyce affair, a staffer may be the partner or lover of another MP who can't keep them in their own office. Sometimes a staffer may be a combination of two or more of those categories or perhaps something quite different, but equally unrelated to the notion of being hired on the basis of job skills.

I've seen all of those appointments, and as you might expect, they never lead to a fully functioning environment. Generally there is mistrust, jealousy and not a lot of competence engaged in undertaking the business of the nation. Even in my own case, I was initially put in place for a range of political reasons unrelated to any ability I might have to advise on portfolio matters.

I'm not sure if Tony was at all surprised when I proved to be capable of doing the job remarkably well. I remember with some level of satisfaction that I was the first person ever to write material for Tony that he didn't amend. Your detractors rarely if ever have a fair view of you and Tony wasn't immune to those feelings, but the fact is that he is an extraordinarily intelligent man – highly educated both scholastically and otherwise – a Rhodes scholar. So, for me it was quite an achievement to be able to write for Tony and do so knowing he'd consider it good enough not to change. He became increasingly reliant on me and appreciated my work and that made leaving him especially hard. Most people want to be where they feel valued – I'm no exception to that.

As a matter of fairness and accuracy, every political office also has a proportion of very competent staffers who add their smarts to the mix. It would be better for Australia if that proportion were somewhat higher.

The first, second and third priority of the staff of every office is the re-election of the MP – this is understandable and defensible. It also means if the MP keeps getting elected, the staff generally keep their jobs.

It's very hard to fire someone from an MP's office because the MP is often concerned what secrets the fired employee might take with them, and with that, the trouble they may make within the party structure once out of the MP's office.

The real problem is not created by the priority of getting the MP re-elected, it's created by the issue of preselection. That is where the party structure determines who their candidate will be for each

My dad, Ernest (Bill), aged twenty-five, with a sugar glider, 1943

Dad in 1943

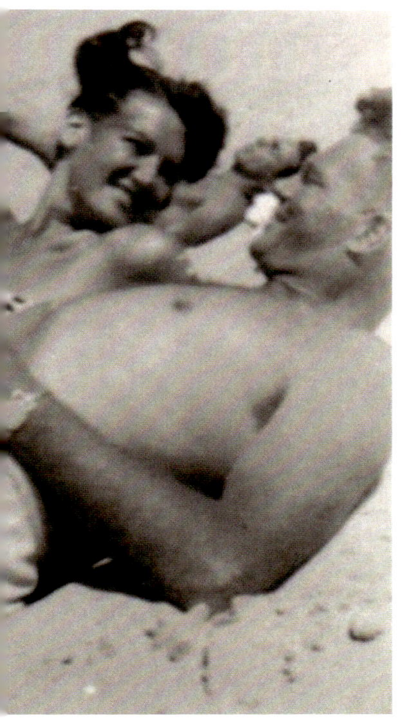

Mum and Dad at the beach, 1955

With Dad, 1980

Rock band days, 1978

Australian Diving Champion 1986

Doing a vox pop, Melbourne, 1998

With Pauline Hanson, 1997

Broadcasting at 2UE, 2011

With Natalie Imbruglia and Nikki Wendt on *First Contact II*, 2016

First Contact, Cape York, 2016

Survivor cast in Vanuatu, 2006 (Tarsha Hosking/Seven Network)

Survivor portrait Vanuatu, 2006 (Tarsha Hosking/Seven Network)

Survivor, competing to recover a sunken chest, Vanuatu, 2006 (Tarsha Hoslking/ Seven Network)

Lisa and I on the set of Channel 7's *Morning Show* with Larry and Kylie, 2018

David and Lisa at home, 2006

David and Lisa in Perth, 2004

Lisa, Henry, David and dogs Lulu and Dinky, 2011

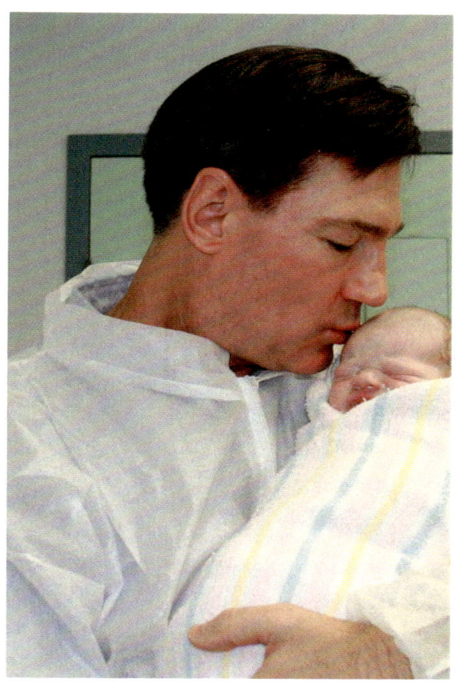

With newborn Henry, 2010

Henry and Albert sleeping, 2012

David, Henry and Albert rescue a kookaburra, 2016

On *I'm a Celebrity Get Me Out of Here!* Reciting a poem while holding a tarantula, Vanuatu, 2018 (Nigel Wright)

The *Hell's Kitchen* Red Team, 2017 (Jeremy Greive)

and every electorate. And that's where a lot of the staff work comes into play, not on policy or assistance to constituents, but making sure their MP keeps winning the preselection held by the party for their electorate, so their boss continues being the candidate at each election. This makes the battle between the factions and party personalities ugly – real ugly. The battle also always entails keeping local members happy and discouraging any potential challengers from within the party.

One occasion that was more typical of stupidity than anything else, but always brings a smile to my face (I'm smiling even now as I type), was a local preselection which was the first to be held for local government in our area. There were two candidates, and rather than focus on the need to win the byelection and get the first ever Liberal endorsed candidate elected to our local council, the whole thing descended into a factional fight. Neither of the candidates were members of a faction, but one was willing to play the game to finally get elected anywhere – this person would have run in an election for a seat warmer if the opportunity had arisen. To this day, I've still never met anyone so hell-bent on being elected to anything, anywhere, anytime.

The other candidate was completely naive but genuine, and although not factionally aligned, probably ideologically centre-right if anything. The other candidate, who likely didn't know what ideology was, let alone have any, aligned with the right wing to ensure the preselection. The right didn't seem to care what that person was or wasn't. The naive candidate came from the biggest local branch, so had good support, including from most of the left, because the right's support was for the other candidate.

By the way, I was never factionally aligned in the Liberal party, though I was considered to be with the left – go figure. Sadly, factional membership is often more about personalities and opportunities than it is about ideological leanings. Numerous people swapped factions, sometimes more than once, simply to get ahead. It disgusted me and still does.

So, this first ever local government preselection was very close on paper, but behind the scenes, it looked bad for the better candidate. However, looking beyond factional lines, I figured it was closer to a tie than an outright loss – one vote changing either way would be needed to make the difference.

Unfortunately for the right faction, I was very quietly dating one of their supposedly solid reliable members, so it went the way it should have. The best candidate won, but arguably, and hence sadly, for the wrong reasons. In fairness to the young lady in question, I'm certain she considered her vote went the right way. My influence just helped her see the best way to vote and helped her make the decision to go against her faction.

If the right's tireless numbers man ever reads this, though it occurred nearly twenty-five years ago, I think it'll be the first time he's ever worked out how his plans went wrong.

It's a grubby business where often the right thing may get done, but it's rare for that to happen merely because it is the right thing to do. Deals upon deals, favours, positions as pay-offs – perhaps it comes as no surprise to you that politics is the dirtiest of all enterprises. I suspect there are Colombian drug cartels with more honour and honesty among members than what is commonly seen within political parties.

The above only scratches the surface of the awful nature of politics, and it was from within this environment that I was, after the fact, expected to be 100 per cent open, and play by rules that didn't exist.

When making the political moves I decided I needed to make, it was impossible to do what I needed to do any way other than the way I did – quietly and secretly. Just as is always the case, all the dirty players cry foul when they're beaten at their own game, in their own no-rules contest. Still, to a lot of people it will be difficult to understand why it was hard for me to leave Tony and ultimately, when I made the decision to go, why I decided I would need to stay on long enough to complete every aspect of my work. I could have just downed tools and walked out, especially since I was certainly burning my bridges because of where I was going. I think that is what most other people would have done. Thinking about it, I know it's hard for a lot of people to understand why someone would do something they would never do themselves.

Pauline Hanson was pressuring me daily to leave Tony. I gave Tony a written resignation, but rather than running out on him, I made it clear I would stay on long enough to finalise everything and prepare matters so they could be easily passed on to whoever replaced me. Tony was sorry I was going, but glad I would stay long enough to get the job done. He gave me a reference that went on glowingly for two pages.

I stayed for over three weeks. That was as long as I could stave off Hanson's demands and just long enough for me to get the job done. I finished up on a Friday night at 7.30 pm – I was the last to leave the office. I left behind a job that was finalised in every way, with all files completed and with substantial written advice attached for whoever filled my role.

Unfortunately, the timing was such that I started as Pauline Hanson's principal advisor on the following Monday, so the fallout was unavoidable and understandable. Yes, I was advising Pauline while I was still with Tony and as unfortunate as that is easily made to look, the fact is I didn't at any stage fail to do my job for Tony throughout that time. I didn't pass on any confidential information nor did I compromise Tony in any way. No secrets went with me. Seriously, there weren't any government secrets – I worked in the education portfolio, not ASIO!

Tony copped it quite a bit when it all became public. I'm sorry for that. He wasn't to know, and the suggestion he should have known was ridiculous. My work was always well done and completed as required – he had no reason to be suspicious. Anyway, what of all the others in Tony's office? What about all the other people I worked with? Is it lost on the knockers that those people didn't notice anything amiss? After all, I was with them virtually all day every day and none of them noticed anything.

As unusual as it no doubt is, the whole time I was creating One Nation and advising Pauline while still with Tony, I was still diligently working for him, and did so right up until the last moment of my last day in his office. Fact is, what I did during that time regarding the creation of Pauline Hanson's One Nation was achieved in my own time – my nights, my weekends, my time off.

There wasn't anything for anyone to notice and so they didn't! As hard as it may be to accept, in my mind I was loyal to Tony and my responsibilities to him, even though I was secretly making a new political party.

On my last day, Tony and I had a sandwich together. Below, also from the Nationwide feature in *The Australian* newspaper on 28 August 2003, entitled, 'The Oldfield Agenda', is an account of those moments, as reported by Megan Saunders.

> It was Friday, May 9, 1997, when David Oldfield and Tony Abbott last sat down together as friends. It was Oldfield's last day working for the rising Liberal Party politician and he was keeping a secret that was political dynamite. Then, over a casual sandwich, Abbott asked a question that took Oldfield by surprise. 'I don't know where he got the idea but he said to me: "You are not going to Pauline Hanson, are you?"' Oldfield recalled yesterday. 'I said: "Tony we have been friends for a long time. I have supported you. I have done everything you wanted me to do. Don't ask me questions I can't answer." He just left it.'

And that is how it happened. Whatever Tony was thinking, he seemed to accept what I said and didn't enquire further. We finished our hasty farewell meal and said goodbye. It would be some twelve years before we'd speak to each other again.

My ideological beliefs forced me from the Liberal Party, but my belief in Tony hadn't been shaken. I had wanted to work for him for the rest of my career; I had pictured him as one day being prime minister with me as a senior personal advisor or perhaps still his private secretary.

However, the areas in which I felt the Howard government was failing caused me to grab hold of the chance to let Australians hear the alternatives. That chance was through the vehicle of Pauline Hanson and convincing her to lead Pauline Hanson's One Nation.

I regret the trouble caused for Tony, but on full examination, it didn't stop him. Before long he was a senior minister and on to leader of government business. Oh, and did I mention he became the prime minister?

I liked and respected Tony. I always have and suspect I always will. Even through all the terrible angst between us during more than a decade where I was seemingly still engaged in Hansonism, I was never able to dislike Tony, though God knows he tempted me to feel that way.

There will always be unreasonable people who refuse to accept any explanation or truly take into account the realities of what occurred, but what I did were simply the actions of a person whose beliefs compelled him to do what he felt to be the right thing.

I was caught in that scenario of trying to accept the things I couldn't change, but trying to change the things I couldn't accept. I chose to try and change what I couldn't accept. At least in my mind (which is where it counts most), doing what I believed to be best, usurped any hold any person or institution might argue they had upon me.

More than anyone else, it is me who lives with those decisions. The only regret I have, that is in anyway sustainable, is that I wasn't able to do more with One Nation – an organisation that is now little more than a personal money-making scheme.

The only betrayal related at all to me is that what I created ultimately let down all those who believed it would make a difference. I'm sorry that happened, but it's hard to picture what more I could have done.

> I very much regret David's decision to leave, although I think it's in his own best interests. David has too much to offer and is too strong a personality to enjoy for long the essentially derivative life of a political staffer.
>
> – The Hon. Tony Abbott MP,
> May 1997

Pauline Hanson and One Nation

David Oldfield is often portrayed as devious and self-serving; a manipulative genius who mercilessly used, then dumped, Pauline Hanson to advance his own political career. But the man I meet in 2015 is driven by something far more potent than personal ambition: deep, heartfelt patriotism.

– Anna Broinowski,
author and documentary filmmaker,
from the 2017 book, *Please Explain*

Pauline Hanson doesn't really exist, at least not in the sense her supporters see her. This is also true for some of her detractors. Clearly, she has a physical form, but what she thinks and believes is so misunderstood and misrepresented as to be no more than an idea in the minds of observers. The real Pauline isn't at all what those who vote for her see, rather, it is as if they have invented a persona that suits their own beliefs and then projected that onto Pauline. She doesn't represent what they think she does and isn't even trying to do anything they'd like her to get done.

It is often said that there is good in everyone – I don't subscribe to that. At the very least, it is something of a balance issue for any thinking person – 2 per cent of good doesn't count for much when put together with 98 per cent of what many would describe as evil.

For example, it is widely understood Adolf Hitler loved children. Indeed, the mother of a friend of mine met Hitler when she was a child and he was very friendly and kind to her, but really, it's Hitler; does his fondness for children mean much in the scheme of things?

It would be remiss of me in this theme not to also note that Hitler's policies were directly responsible for the deaths of countless children and for making millions of others into orphans, so any good there? It would seem the fondness Hitler had for children was momentary and selective; indeed, he used the children of Germany to his own ends.

I suppose it's a Christian thing this 'there is good in everyone', but I'd argue that when given context and any fair evaluation of outcomes, the Christians have got this one wrong.

Before you all go running off at the mouth telling people I compared Pauline Hanson to Hitler, that isn't what I'm doing and if that's what you do, you'll be misrepresenting me – something I'm quite used to by the way. I'm putting forward a case that the amount of good in a person may be so minuscule and of so little actual impact, that it really counts for nothing. In making that case I'm using an example that everyone will understand.

The balance, if you like, will be in what I'll put to you about what I saw of Pauline and you can make up your own mind. For me, in the scheme of things, it's hard to find any redeeming features in Pauline. That is to say any redeeming features that come even close to compensating for Pauline's mindset. Here goes, you decide.

It's appropriate to set the stage by explaining how I met Pauline and how Pauline Hanson's One Nation came to exist. As has been suggested, it was at a nightclub come restaurant in Canberra called the Grange. It was a favourite destination for politicians and their staff, so you could pretty much see anyone there. It was the place to meet, and yes, in a sense, it was something of a pick-up joint, though a very nice establishment at that time.

I've noted the Grange was the place to meet, so am I inferring a lot of happy times, occur between those working at Parliament House? You betcha! Parliament House was (don't know if it has changed) a hotbed of affairs and general promiscuity, especially among staffers, and of course politicians as well, and all those who interact with both. It's a high-pressure environment with, in those days, lots of alcohol, lots of playing hard, huge egos and the aphrodisiac of power, so it's no surprise its pastimes ran along the lines of those of Sodom and Gomorrah.

That's not to say all the married people were unfaithful, because it's decidedly unfair to the strong-willed hold outs who weren't, but it's accurate to say the place was pretty much as you'd expect, when being realistic about how humans act in such environments – like animals on the Discovery Channel!

It would be hypocritical if I didn't note I had fun in Canberra too, but no differently to anywhere else I'd been. I didn't feel the 'power' effects I'm describing – I was just myself as I'd always been, and I wasn't ever in any kind of relationship, so the matter of unfaithfulness never related to me.

I've seen and heard many things regarding the fervour with which pollies attempted to satisfy their urges, but one of the more memorable came from a parliament security guard I knew well and still know to this day.

He, in company with a colleague, happened to burst in on two very high profile parliamentarians (one a former Cabinet minister) who were, in classic fashion, doing it on the desk. Personally, I think the lounge is more comfortable, but people of power get a kick out of the desk. Ahh, the passion of politics. For the record, I've never done the desk thing – I've never felt that need.

The female in this daring desk driving duo managed to accidentally trip the silent duress button which immediately summoned security who burst through the door to find, she, with her skirt up around her waist and he, with his pants restricting his ankles but not restricting the animalistic enthusiasm of his thrusting. Both of these sexual adventurers were married, neither were young, but there they were, going for it like a couple of teenagers in the backseat of a car. If I seem to make it all sound tawdry, that's because it is – no romance, not in love, just a couple in midlife crisis riding a desk.

The male was reputedly someone his party would enlist when the mission required emotional manipulation of a lonely middle-aged female, who would naturally fall for his worldly charms.

If you mistakenly think the above example is something of a one-off of what's going on behind the closed doors of parliamentary offices, think again. Take the widely reported situation of Barnaby Joyce, which cost him the leadership of the National Party and the position of Deputy Prime Minister.

The seats of power were often pounding the desks in Parliament House – politicians instinctively engaged in primal behaviour, screwing each other, rather than constituents and the country, just for a change.

There was a time, when as a society, we expected more of our leaders than the transgressions expected of others. Do we no longer expect better from our leaders, or do we no longer see politicians as leaders?

It was on the night of Pauline's maiden speech that I met her. That afternoon I'd watched a bit of her speech live over the Parliament House monitors. I saw perhaps half of it while I was working, pausing now and then when walking past the screen in our office. The speech itself was crude and poorly written and Pauline's delivery didn't improve it, but elements of the content were interesting and, in some cases, hard to argue against.

Pauline said things a lot of Australians had been waiting to hear. It didn't matter how badly she said them, indeed the author of the speech had anticipated how badly she'd make the pitch and incorporated the line, 'I come here not as a polished politician'. Perhaps that one line encapsulated much of Pauline's appeal: she wasn't one of the establishment, just an ordinary Australian.

One of the most interesting aspects here is the acceptance by the listeners that these were Pauline's thoughts, Pauline's words, Pauline's feelings of despair for her beloved Australia, whereas in fact all that belonged to the author of the speech.

That night, as she sat with her secretary in a corner of the Grange, a young political apparatchik, who I promised never to name, was almost climbing on her table spewing bile and hate and calling her every bad word there is and more. The fellow is someone I know, but he isn't, nor was he, a friend of mine and I wasn't in his company when he verbally assaulted Pauline. I was just there, near the bar, like so many others.

It wasn't the first time I'd stepped between a man and a woman in such circumstances and it wasn't the last either. I pulled him away and told him to leave her alone and then I apologised to her and expressed that it was wrong for him to speak to her in such a way. That was how I met Pauline Hanson. It was a simple case of being present when she was attacked and stopping it, something that any reasonable person should have done.

Understandably, Pauline took an immediate like to me. She was, in many respects 'a damsel in distress', and I had come to her rescue.

I only had to catch up with Pauline once more to conclude that she was completely lost. She really had no idea what to do and just shunted along, out of her depth, day after day. Back then, I took the view she was well meaning, but not very bright. She would look at me with eyes that gave away the fact she really didn't have a clue.

My initial thought on how best to use Pauline politically was to tie her into the Liberal Party as a kind of informal right-wing ally who articulated things others wouldn't, and to feed preferences back to the party, not unlike the arrangement the Liberals had with the Democratic Labor Party (DLP) so long ago.

To those naive to matters of human behaviour, 'using Pauline' likely seems a tad wrong, but the reality is most if not all people use others to achieve things. This may be done through coercion, sometimes through deception, and often with the expectation that said use may bring reward, and hence those used may be utilised in a kind of voluntary manner.

Of course, whatever a person is trying to achieve, how they go about it is reasonably determined to be largely right, or very wrong, by virtue of their intentions and planned outcome. In many respects it just comes down to the ends justifying the means. Machiavelli didn't say that, by the way, so the statement shouldn't be linked to the simple though ruthless and self-interest-based behaviour attributed to Machiavellianism.

I don't subscribe to the view that one may do anything to achieve an aim if one's aim is in itself, good. The first problem being that in most things what is seen as good by some, is seen as bad by others. Yes, I just admitted that because I think something is good and right and fair doesn't necessarily mean it is. The same matter will be seen completely the opposite by another. The notion of good triumphing over evil is often merely subjective in that to those who lost, their good was triumphed over by evil. There are perhaps very few issues where one can definitively determine what is good and what is bad and have the majority agree. There are perhaps no matters at all where everyone will agree absolutely that something is good or bad.

Take the example of paedophilia. I'm hopeful the vast majority of people would take the position that dealing sexually with children is amongst the very worst of crimes and perpetrators should be dealt with strongly, to say the least. However, even with this issue, that should be so straight forward, there are those who argue having sex with children is just another form of sexuality.

My understanding of their position doesn't alter my disagreement or anger about such people, and in this case, I use the term 'people' somewhat loosely. Those who deal sexually with children are, in my view, amongst the lowest creatures on earth. I'm sure they cannot be rehabilitated because I'm sure it's in their sexual orientation.

In fairness (I'm always fair about why people are how they are), it's possible Pauline was okay, or at least a little okay and maybe even a little well-meaning at the start, but as soon as anything got even a little bit tough or something was required of her, she struggled.

One of the greatest difficulties in working with people in public life is when they get the idea they're of vastly greater importance to the planet than they really are. It is often seen with 'celebrities', many of whom actually get to a point where they think they're above being spoken to by ordinary people.

I think this is most apparent when the person involved isn't very smart and perhaps is compounded by not previously having achieved much. Perhaps the overnight star who comes from nothing and suddenly finds themselves in unbelievable demand, when only days or weeks before, they'd been a grey, anonymous member of society shuffling down the street and not rating a first look, let alone a second.

Pauline was a bit like this, but she wasn't on her own. When One Nation won eleven seats in the Queensland state election in 1998, I did my very best to try to make those members understand they weren't any different or better than they were the day before the election, but I wasted my time. A few of them had come from respectable positions, but many had never amounted to anything and suddenly they were important for the first time in their lives. And the last time too, because public life didn't last long for any of them; it truly was fifteen minutes of fame they could never extend.

Those working closest with Pauline soon came to realise she wasn't the Messiah, Joan of Arc or anything along those lines. She wasn't going to save anyone or anything, but we were stuck with it, me more than anyone. I'd started it all and in doing so raised unrealistically the hopes of millions of Australians. I had to do what I could with what I had, which was Pauline.

I used to say of Pauline, 'A women who has never been so much as the captain of a primary school netball team, is now heading the third most powerful political party in the country.'

It was madness; I felt Pauline was never up to the job and failed miserably day after day. The constant in the perils of Pauline was always Pauline herself. It seemed to me she would always blame those around her, but those around her have changed over the years, whereas it is she who has continued to preside over every mess. The only blame Pauline would ever accept for herself was in making the mistake of trusting people. Yes, that's right, Pauline has never made a mistake in her whole life except for trusting people, who then made the mistakes that brought her undone ...

Let me take you back to 1997. As I'd started to explain, my initial thoughts on Pauline were that she was well-meaning but completely out of her depth.

My expectation following the election of John Howard as PM at the 1996 election was that the Liberals would naturally address matters including immigration and multiculturalism, yet they weren't touching those issues. To say I was disappointed would be a huge understatement. Australia failing to be a lot more picky about who was let in, and the craziness of multiculturalism, were very serious matters to me, very serious. As far as I was concerned, much of what was wrong with

Australia and where things would go wrong from here could be traced back to Whitlam and Grasby and the failure of the Fraser Government to reverse those policies. At the start of Howard's reign, there was no indication he would do any more than Fraser. I liked John Howard, but as they say, 'Not happy John'.

Just to be sure of not being misunderstood, even though I'll no doubt be again misrepresented and misquoted and quoted out of context, I'm against multiculturalism, but I'm not against Australians being made up of many different races.

So, I decided Pauline could be recruited, so to speak, to be like a very conservative-ish wing of the Liberal Party and say all the things the Howard Government clearly didn't have the balls to say. I was hopeful the natural progression would be for the Liberals to then move closer to the sort of things Pauline would say and over time re-occupy that territory.

I started to explain my idea to Tony (as in Abbott, as in future prime minister), but I didn't get far. I recollect I got to about, 'Tony, I've met Pauline Hanson and I think we could use her ...' At that point, Tony stopped me and said, 'Stay away from her Dave, stay away from her.' He may have said mate rather than Dave, but you get the point.

I really like Tony and I had a habit of doing what Tony said, but this time around I decided he was wrong. Hanson was too much not to be taken advantage of, so, I decided I'd have to do something without the Liberal Party.

I knew what had to be done, but I didn't know what Pauline had in mind. Pauline had no idea about parties or how politics worked administratively. In fairness, Pauline was just a very simple person, unworldly, unaffected and without the vaguest notion of how things work. She knew the most basic things she needed to know to get by and in that, she wasn't on her own.

The difference between Pauline and so many other people is that she had, by a series of events, not in her plans and beyond her control, been thrust into the national spotlight and was expected to have the answers to all our problems. Of course, she had few answers. She was just angry about her lot in life and not even really able to articulate that, let alone the policy platform to reclaim Australia that her supporters expected.

People saw in Pauline something she never was, and they immediately placed her on a pedestal and expected of her things that were never a part of her thinking. Many typical conservative voters supporting Pauline just took for granted that she thought as they did on every subject.

An example of this was the issue of abortion. In early 1998, Pauline got the party into hot water while in Toowoomba when she was asked about abortion and she left no doubt she backed abortion 100 per cent. There was outrage: how could it be that our Pauline could think like that? How could she be so evil as to support the murder of unborn innocents?

Regardless of one's view of abortion, the side Pauline took was not what was assumed by her conservative backers – they were wrong about her, and not just on this. They assumed she strongly supported issues that had never been raised because they projected their own conservative views onto her despite not having any actual understanding of where Pauline stood.

For the most part, I got us out of the abortion problem and it didn't spread from Toowoomba, as many had feared, especially the local candidates for the coming Queensland state election, who were horrified at the potential impact. I spun the matter to have been taken out of context and that Pauline supported the existing laws that made abortion illegal; it was the best that could be done under the circumstances.

I also made sure Pauline never again uttered a word about abortion, so that problem was effectively behind us. But imagine how the religious right would have stormed against us if they'd discovered Pauline was an atheist. Like so many beliefs wrongly attributed to Pauline, it was apparently beyond question that she must be a staunch Christian. Ah … no.

It's worth backing up here and looking at how Pauline got elected, because it's a terrible mistake for anyone to think it was something that went according to plan.

Pauline Hanson had been selected as the Liberal candidate for the federal electorate of Oxley. It was a strongly held Labor safe seat with the Liberal Party having no expectation whatsoever of winning. Had they thought there was any real chance, they wouldn't have selected Pauline in the first place. Hers was a campaign to support votes for the Senate. Pauline was a filler not expected to even come close.

The Liberals hadn't held government since Bob Hawke beat them in 1983. They should have won office in 1993, but were stopped in their tracks by the craziness of John Hewson and his GST that even he couldn't plausibly explain. During the disaster of the 1993 campaign, I worked in the GST information centre at Liberal HQ in Sydney. Several times I wandered upstairs to tell the director that people were not buying the GST – we were losing them hand over fist. On one such occasion I was told, 'The leader knows what he's doing and things are on track, there's no changing anything.' To which I said, 'So if we were an army and attacked from behind, you're saying we couldn't change direction?' The answer was, 'Correct. We're going forward, there will be no change in direction.'

And, as they say, the rest is history. The history being that the Hewson-led Liberals were defeated by Paul Keating, but the reality is that they were defeated by John Hewson and the nonsense of trying to regain office with a tax as central policy – madness. I'm sure John Hewson has a great deal of expertise, however, none of it happens to be related to politics or public affairs. If the Liberals hadn't been so desperate after the multiple failed attempts to regain government, with John Howard and Andrew Peacock taking turns as leader, they likely wouldn't have selected Hewson to lead the assault in 1993.

It's worth noting here that when it comes to a sales pitch for an election, it's easy to sell fear and damn near impossible to sell bravery. You can sell fear all day long, but you can't give away bravery for free. John Hewson tried to get Australians to be brave and accept a new tax that, despite being its architect, he couldn't plausibly explain himself. Paul Keating simply played the fear card again and again, and that's what people grabbed hold of. The fear offered freely was more acceptable than a solution that came with a price.

The other lesson here is that in public affairs, messages have to be simple enough so as not to require explanation. Identify the buttons to push and just keep pushing the buttons. Once you have to stop and make long-winded explanations, you lose people.

By 1996, the Liberals had gone back to someone they understood. John Howard was the leader again and there was no way he was going to lose the un-lose-able election like Hewson.

Yep, un-lose-able. The 1993 election has always been referred to as 'un-lose-able'. Syphilis riding on a donkey could have won the 1993 election if it hadn't been saddled with Hewson's GST.

John Howard played it safe – nothing outside the playbook, and he scored a huge victory that rivalled the Liberal landslides of 1949 and 1975. After the great victory of 1996, John Howard was a hero and Liberal Party headquarters was full of geniuses. But the truth is, the 1996 result was close to what the 1993 result would have been had the campaign been fought traditionally and without Hewson and his 'brave' GST.

In 1996, the Coalition likely won a few extra seats than they would have in 1993 because after another three years of Paul Keating and Labor, the country was even more desperate than they had been when Hewson screwed it up. There is a saying, and I don't know who said it first, but it goes like this, 'Oppositions don't win elections, governments lose them'. Such would have been the case in 1993 and ultimately was the case in 1996. No matter what a government does, even when they're doing a good job, there comes a time when people want change, so they vote the government out. Makes no sense, but after all we're dealing with people, and people in the mix often precludes good sense from staying in charge.

The same thing was done to John Howard in 2007. There wasn't much that made real sense to change the government, but the Liberals had been in for eleven years and there was the appearance they were out of ideas, that John Howard was tired, and Kevin Rudd looked young, new and fresh. Of course that didn't end well, and Kevin Rudd finished up being reported as an ear-wax chewing, narcissistic, micromanaging foul-tempered egomaniac – not so fresh and nice apparently, but perhaps still more popular than his successor Julia Gillard, who was then succeeded briefly by Kevin Rudd again. Oh my goodness, those were the days.

In all of that, the really interesting thing is that without John Hewson's miserable failure, John Howard would never have been given another chance and his career high point would have been deemed to have occurred back when he served in the Fraser government. Funny how things turn out; of Keating, Hewson, Howard, Rudd and Gillard, it is clearly Howard who stands out as the most successful and respected. In 1993, you wouldn't have put a dollar on John Howard's future and yet he became our second longest serving prime minister, a record I suspect he may hold forever.

Many know Pauline Hanson was the Liberal candidate for Oxley in 1996, but I'm not sure how broadly the public understands that if Pauline had actually reached election day and still been the Liberal candidate, that is where it would have finished. Pauline wouldn't have won Oxley as a Liberal; there'd have been no maiden speech, no night at the Grange, no meeting me, and no Pauline Hanson's One Nation.

There's a bit to explain about all that; in fact, Pauline would say, 'Please explain'. And she'd need to, because as crazy as it might seem to some, she doesn't understand the manner of her own making. Here's how it happened.

Pauline is the Liberal candidate in a seat that won't be won by the Liberals. There's just a local campaign without much oversight from head office because such resources are focused on marginal seats that can be won. Pauline's campaign manager is doing all the hard yards. Part way into the campaign, a letter signed by Pauline makes its way to the local paper. The letter complains about Aborigines:

Equal justice for all

Black deaths in custody seem to be Robert Tickner's latest outcry.

Pity that as much media coverage or political grandstanding is not shown for white deaths in custody.

As for Tickner's statement that Aborigines should not go to jail because apparently it is not working: imagine what type of country this would be to live if Aborigines didn't go to jail for their crimes.

One of these men was serving a 12-year sentence and it wasn't just a speeding fine.

Can you imagine then if we had equality, then we would have no prisoners at all.

The indigenous people of this country are as much responsible for their actions as any other colour or race in this country.

The problem is that politicians in all their profound wisdom have and are causing a racism problem.

I would be the first to admit that, not that many years ago the Aborigines were treated wrongly but in trying to correct this they have gone too far.

I don't feel responsible for the treatment of Aboriginal people in the past because I had no say but my concern now is for the future.

How can you expect this race to help themselves when government showers them with money, facilities and opportunities that only these people can obtain no matter how minute the indigenous blood that is flowing through their veins, and this is what is causing racism.

Until government wake up to themselves and start looking at equality not colour then we might start to work together as one.

Pauline Hanson, Ipswich
– Letter to *The Queensland Times,*
6 January 1996

The Liberals believe they're going to suffer by being tarnished with what are considered racial slurs and so to cover themselves, they make a big noise in making an example of Pauline. They make it clear her views are not those of the Liberal Party and to remove any doubt and possible damage across Queensland, or even nationally, they disendorse Pauline. Liberal polling shows they're not anywhere near winning the seat, so they can write her off in an apparent act of demonstrating high principles. This happens at a time in the campaign timetable where it's not possible to replace Pauline with a new candidate and hence there will not be a Liberal candidate running in Oxley.

However, the ballot papers have already been printed and Pauline is still shown as a Liberal, so she gets the Liberal voters as well as Labor voters who liked what Pauline was saying and could now vote for her because she's actually an independent. That combined with the general swing against Keating and the appearance Pauline was dumped for standing up and speaking her mind on an issue that crossed party lines in a largely working-class electorate, was enough for Pauline to get elected. Without the combination of those events and the huge level of media that came as a consequence, none of which was anyone's plan, but rather a series of reactions, Pauline wouldn't have been elected and that would likely have been the last anyone would have heard of her.

The next that came of Pauline in any major sense was her maiden speech. That garnered national publicity on an unprecedented scale and support poured in from across the nation. However, John Pasquarelli, Pauline's advisor and general handler at the time, has always claimed he wrote the maiden speech. As someone who knows Pauline's abilities and mindset as they were at that time better than anyone, I believe Pasquarelli.

The whole time I directed Pauline, she didn't want to write a single word or be involved in working with anyone else to write anything. It was impossible to get her to even read, as in check anything written for her or put out in her name. Whenever I wrote a press release, I had to read it to her like a parent reads a story to a child – I kid you not. I had to make things interesting for her, entertain her, or she wouldn't pay attention for a second. I had to do it that way because initially when I'd leave something for her to read, she just wouldn't do it. She'd read the first sentence and then look like she was thinking about her next nail appointment, but later complain she hadn't been told what we were doing.

So the famous Hanson maiden speech, said to contain what so many wanted to say yet said by Pauline, wasn't her work; she was merely the mouthpiece for someone else's view of Australia.

Let's take it a step further back. It's my understanding, from numerous conversations and contacts, that the letter to the Queensland Times, that got Pauline disendorsed by the Liberal Party, resulting in her election, was written by her campaign manager, Morrie Marsden.

There is a pattern of behaviour from Pauline that tends to uphold that Marsden did write that letter. Consider this, Marsden writes the letter that leads to her election, Pasquarelli writes the maiden speech that captures the nation and I write the speech that launches Pauline Hanson's One Nation on 11 April 1997 – what did Pauline contribute? She contributed a symbol without substance; she was the mouthpiece of the ideas and ideology of others. She played a role that was written and scripted, and just like a movie, the fans fell in love with the actress as if the role she played was real and as if the character she seemed to portray was her.

Pauline's role was helped along by Pauline being an apparently vulnerable woman who was courageously standing up for her beliefs. But the truth was that she wasn't so much vulnerable as incompetent and inarticulate.

Then there is the matter of the party itself and how it came into being, something of which I'm the most informed as I was at the centre of it all. It was initiated by me and brought about through me.

> I clearly recall the day Pauline Hanson made her famous maiden speech as the new federal Member for Oxley.
>
> The following morning David Oldfield phoned me to say that by chance he had met Pauline the previous evening at a Canberra club.
>
> A couple of weeks later, David told me he had counselled Pauline and overcome strong influences by various people keen that Pauline should not start a political party.
>
> It was David who explained to Pauline the reasons why a party was the best way for her to influence political change in Australia and why having a party was the only way to clearly identify candidates on ballot papers. David knew candidates had to be associated with Pauline's rapidly growing popularity and profile and it could only be done through a party and the essential link that would then be made through ballot papers on election day.
>
> Having convinced Pauline that creating a political party was the only way, David soon introduced me to Pauline as a person who could create and manage the administration of the new party. Not too many days

> passed before the three of us had a meeting in Sydney and discussed the roles we could each perform.
>
> Pauline would be the party's leader and the party figurehead, I would handle the marketing and administration and David would handle media and the political aspects of the party.
>
> That meeting led to the birth of Pauline Hanson's One Nation, and the whole idea and need for that to happen started with David Oldfield.
>
> – David Ettridge,
> co-founder Pauline Hanson's One Nation,
> April 2018

I took a controversial independent (Pauline Hanson) and added an administrator (David Ettridge), coopted existing supporters and formed a political party using Pauline's name so there wouldn't be any confusion as to what it all was. I co-founded Pauline Hanson's One Nation with Pauline and David Ettridge, but have no doubt, the basis of what the party stood for, albeit often misunderstood and misportrayed, came from my beliefs. I ran past Pauline what I wanted to do, but her position was merely one of agreement and going along.

Of course Pauline would remember it differently, but the fact is, she was a vehicle driven by me, to carry what I wanted to convey. My apologies for how poor she was at articulating even the most simple of matters, but she was the only way.

> Like myself, David Oldfield is a true believer in Australia, the nation state and its identity. By guiding Pauline Hanson's One Nation ideologically, he strengthened and built the party without regard for any personal benefits for himself.
>
> David Oldfield understands the dangers of multiculturalism and inappropriate immigration and has never stopped speaking out on those issues.
>
> Like all true believers, David has paid the price for his patriotism. There are no rewards now for defending our Western way of life; rather, those who take the pragmatic stand for modern civilisation, are persecuted.

> Should we ultimately lose this battle, history will erase the great efforts and sacrifices of those such as David Oldfield, who worked against the odds, to make a difference.
>
> – Robyn Spencer,
> former Victorian convener
> and immigration spokesperson for One Nation,
> May 2018

Pauline was the party's greatest strength in a sense, but also its greatest weakness. It couldn't have been done without her and equally, it was mostly unintentionally thwarted by her.

By the same token, without me, the party would never have been formed. Pauline had been convinced to remain an independent. Even the fellow who started the national support movement was utterly 100 per cent against forming a party. I had to overcome a lot of entrenched opposition, including from Pauline herself, to be successful in making Pauline Hanson's One Nation a reality.

Even the name was something I had to push past Pauline because, like most people, she didn't understand the need of 'branding' for the purposes of candidate recognition. Launching any new product without a fortune in funds for marketing to raise brand awareness is doomed to failure, but attach a name and face that everyone knows, and suddenly the product is easily seen.

The product, in a sense was the faceless unknowns we put on ballot papers, but the fact they were unknowns was overcome by the party's name, because when supporters saw Pauline Hanson's One Nation on the ballot paper, they didn't need to identify anything else to decide their vote. And so, that is how the name came about and yet it took Pauline more than a decade to finally see the importance of attaching her own name as the means of identifying where to mark the ballot paper.

Even today, One Nation could not effectively exist without Pauline, and some might say it cannot progress with her either. Something that will make its opposition happy is the knowledge that One Nation has no long-term future; it will never evolve beyond Pauline. When she's gone, so is One Nation.

Many reading this may immediately say, 'Hang on, Pauline Hanson's One Nation had four senators elected in 2016, surely they are on the rise. Oldfield is just suffering from a case of sour grapes.'

That's not an unreasonable position to reach. It's what I'd expect from anyone reading headlines and not understanding the numbers and the intricacies behind how the numbers stack up, or how they collapse; and most people don't. When it comes to conservative movements such as the things on which PHON was based, almost everyone gets it wrong. It's not really your fault, you've just been misled – imagine that.

Supposed expert commentators, journalists, other politicians and those referred to as political operators, they almost always get it wrong. I saw that with every PHON success. It was as if they just couldn't grasp how it was being done – not even after it was done.

I remember the chief political reporter for the Courier Mail telling me, just before the 1998 Queensland state election, that if PHON had a single candidate elected, he'd run around Brisbane's Queen Street Mall naked.

In that election a few weeks later, PHON won eleven seats, the first election the party ever contested. I'm still waiting for that 'expert' chief political reporter to do so much as a single lap, let alone the eleven laps he owes me.

Let me raise just one name: Donald Trump. How many 'experts, saw that coming? I'll chuck in Brexit for good measure. Both are simply what I'll call 'Hanson syndrome', expressed in different parts of the world and utterly rejected as possibilities by those who were 'supposed' to know.

The population at large is increasingly reliant on just basic information or results, without any background or details. Results aren't near half of the story – it is the means by which the answers or outcomes are reached that completes stories and constitutes real knowledge.

The 2016 success in the Senate for PHON wasn't the huge resurgence in the party's support that was generally reported by the media – that was just the basis for an easy way to put together a headline. The fact is the outcome occurred through a set of unique circumstances. One must not only examine failure to learn, but also success, because often your success isn't related to your efforts as much as you'd like to think, and indeed, as you'd like to have others think as well. It is too easy for most people to just take the win without ever caring how it happened, but if you want it to happen again, you must look at exactly how things came to be.

The votes secured by PHON in the Senate in the 2016 federal election were proportionally less than half of those received in the Senate in 1998. The nationwide Senate vote for PHON in 2016 was a touch over 593,000 and in 1998 it was a bit over 1,007,000 – a huge difference that is even greater when taking into account the increase in the voting population between the two elections. In 1998 there were 11,584,843 voters, but by 2016 the number of voters had grown to 14,406,706, an increase close to 25 per cent.

In terms of percentages nationally, the formal votes cast for PHON in 1998 made up 8.99 per cent of the votes, but in 2016, formal votes cast for PHON just touched 4.3 per cent. In simple terms, PHON in 2016 had less than half the votes they had in 1998. That's hardly a 'resurgence'! Even with Pauline herself as the Senate candidate for Queensland, where she received 9.19 per cent of the vote in 2016, that was nowhere near the 14.9 per cent received in 1998 by a PHON candidate who was barely known.

New South Wales is perhaps an even better example as the 2016 PHON Senate candidate received just 4.1 per cent of the vote compared to the 1998 result which gave PHON 9.6 per cent of the Senate votes. No resurgence there either, or anywhere else, as the comparison of results across all Australian states turns up similar outcomes.

And here is where it gets easy for people to be misled as to how it came about and what it all means because in 1998 only one PHON candidate was elected to the Senate, yet in 2016 PHON received four senators. How can it be that PHON could get four times as many people elected in 2016 when the party received less than half the support? A perfect storm for PHON caused through a double dissolution election called by Malcolm Turnbull and a change to the way voting occurs for the Senate. Both were hugely helpful to PHON and other small political parties. The double dissolution meant all senators were up for election, instead of half, which is the usual number for a general election. This meant the number of votes needed to get a senator elected was, quite simply, halved.

Double dissolution elections are anything but common. There have been only seven in our nation's history and the last one before 2016 was almost thirty years earlier, in 1987.

However, perhaps of even more consequence for smaller political parties, were the changes to how to vote for the Senate that occurred just before the 2016 election and hence that election was the first where these changes came into effect. The essentially secretive preferences deals where parties allocated your preferences based on you simply voting 1 in the box were done away with, so for the first time, preferences were only allocated for the Senate by the voters actually doing it themselves. If you didn't allocate preferences, your vote just exhausted (died) and that was it, as opposed to previously, where for the most part, political parties passed your vote on as a preference to whomever they'd done deals with. The result is, as candidates are eliminated in the progressive count, their votes are eliminated with them and the number of votes needed to get elected becomes less and less.

Prior to 2016, to be elected to the Senate required each candidate to reach a particular number of votes (usually a bit under 15 per cent) which didn't ever change, so you either had enough votes outright and were elected, or you sat waiting for preferences, directed by predetermined party deals, to flow to you. Because of those all-important changes that first saw the light of day in the Senate election of 2016, the last positions for the Senate in each state would go to candidates with nowhere near what would have normally been required. It just gets down to whoever has the most votes among those, who in theory, didn't have enough votes to begin with.

And that's how PHON got four senators elected in 2016 – not because of any resurgence in support, but rather because of a double dissolution combined with first-time changes to the way preferences were allocated and the way the count for the Senate was undertaken.

Picture this, three of the four PHON candidates elected to the Senate in 2016 secured around a quarter or less than the votes that would have been required without the extraordinary differences to the voting system that met the electorate in that election.

Even Pauline Hanson would likely not have been elected without the double dissolution and the changes to preferences – she would have sat awaiting preferences that would never arrive because the other political parties would have directed their preferences elsewhere, just as they always had in the past.

Don't get me wrong, the changes to preference allocation were something long overdue that I support absolutely. Political parties should never have been able to direct preferences to whomever they liked in a manner largely unknown to voters. But the point remains, it was changes to the system that allowed PHON to be successful in the 2016 election despite having less than half the votes secured in 1998 when PHON was unquestionably at its peak. There was no resurgence for Pauline Hanson's One Nation, but gee it sure looked that way if you didn't understand the system and all you had to go on were the results and the commentary of lazy, uninformed 'experts'.

Sorry if you found all those facts tedious. To be frank, I found writing them quite tedious, and that's generally how facts are – they can seem boring, oh, and a terrible annoyance if they get in the way of the story people would like to tell, and so a lot of 'experts' just ignore them. Taking in results is easy, though often it's an entirely different matter altogether to fully understand how those results came about.

On the matter of sour grapes, is that arguably an affliction from which I suffer? Well, it's usually taken to mean that a person takes a negative attitude toward something simply because they cannot have it themselves and it's easy to see how some would like to apply that to me. But, for what it's worth, mine was never a desire for power or fame, it was always a matter of being angry about what was being done to my country and wanting to do something about that. I know now that was somewhat naive of me.

Oldfield's enemies claim he operates inside an amoral, emotion-free zone, driven by a clinical obsession with power. They are wrong.

> Descended from two generations of military heroes, Oldfield sees himself as a patriotic warrior fighting an ideological war.
>
> – Anna Broinowski,
> author and documentary filmmaker,
> from the 2017 book, *Please Explain*

I noted previously that PHON has a use-by date, that it dies with Pauline. But how long might that be? By the time Pauline's Senate term finishes in 2022 she'll be sixty-eight years old. Will she stand for another six-year term? In my opinion, as long as the adulation and prominence last I expect Pauline will keep going, so probably yes.

A couple of weeks before the 2019 federal election, I appeared on the ABC's 7.30 and when asked about Pauline Hanson's One Nation's prospects in the forthcoming election, I said that the best they could hope for was a single seat in the Senate in Queensland with no wins anywhere else in Australia. And that is exactly how it turned out – only Pauline's candidate for the senate in Queensland, Malcolm Roberts, was elected, but only just, having secured only 10 per cent of the vote, a long way short of a traditional quota, and success only achieved through the benefit of the changed system.

Does Pauline have a chance to win again in 2022 when she is up for re-election? It's likely, and if she's positioned herself to get Coalition preferences at that time, I expect her chances to be re-elected are almost assured.

Elsewhere, the simple maths points to the potential for wins here and there in the New South Wales and Western Australian state parliaments, and we've just seen that with Mark Latham recently elected as the PHON candidate for the New South Wales Legislative Council.

After the 1999 election, the way voting is conducted in the New South Wales upper house also changed and this meant that the number two on the ticket with Mark Latham was also elected, even though the support in 2019 was only about the same as it had been in 1999. Again, PHON had benefitted from electoral changes rather than a surge in support.

One way or another, the time will come when Pauline no longer stands in the Federal Parliament, and that is where Pauline Hanson's One Nation will effectively come to an end. That said, Pauline has tried her hand at the New South Wales Legislative Council before, so don't be surprised if she turns up as a candidate in 2023, joining Mark Latham at the halfway point in his eight-year term, or replaces her candidate elected in the 2019 federal election for the second half of his term. Asking a sitting Senator to stand down for her would be true to form.

Whatever the next few years holds for Pauline and her party, and whichever parliament Pauline is in, don't expect any different to what has already been seen – they have no capacity or ability to bring about any real change and without another double dissolution, there won't be any federal parliamentary members of PHON outside Queensland.

I started the story of Pauline Hanson and One Nation by considering whether or not there is good in everyone, and if there is, does just a little bit really count for very much if anything at all when it comes down to compensating for the bad. I suspect Pauline is the product of her environment and in that, her experiences and how she dealt with what has impacted her life. Nothing unusual there as that is mostly how we're all shaped. Some of us find understanding in what we're dealt. We accept our contribution, as it is, to things that go wrong in our lives and we temper our outlook through taking responsibility, understanding the needs of others, and through the use of context and perspective. Others, however, live their lives as eternal victims who have been unjustly persecuted at every turn; never accept any level of their own fault in what befalls them; never see another's point of view and think everyone they meet may take something from them.

While I'm acutely aware of various things in Pauline's life that likely made her as I believe her to be, based on what I saw of her first hand, to put those here would be unfair to her because they would just be my evaluations of what made the Pauline Hanson I knew. In the way of quite personal matters, I offer the following with reference to Pauline, and perhaps you will choose to come to your own conclusions.

I told you that soon after meeting Pauline I noted she was not very intelligent, but I presumed her to be likely well-meaning. It wasn't long before a range of issues arose that, as far as I'm concerned, demonstrated her to be perhaps anything but well-meaning. Each day I hoped for more from her, just a little more, but each day she moved me further away from being able to see her as a person who should ever be in any position of responsibility for the lives of others.

It's accurate to say I love animals, all animals, but especially dogs, horses and birds – parrots in particular. Part, not all, but part of how I form judgements of people comes from how they are with animals. I'm of the view one can tell a lot about a person by their care for or interest in animals and how they treat animals in general.

Pauline had a little herd of horses on her property – six or seven as I recollect. She didn't do anything with them as such, they were essentially pets. When I stayed at her house, I used to whistle them up and hand feed them treats. One morning, I popped out to whistle up my horsey friends and they didn't appear. They were nowhere to be seen. Pauline had decided they ate too much grass and she could make a few extra bucks by having some cows. It's not something I would have done, but fair enough.

To have an animal in the first place is to take responsibility for their life. In 2007 when my wife Lisa brought home a Jack Russell puppy named Lulu, she told me we were looking after her. When I asked for how long, she replied about sixteen years. Lulu, who I love so very much, has so far lived through cancer, the amputation of a leg, snake bite and a host of other close calls – fortunately, she is with us still.

Horses, like dogs and other pets, need somewhere to go if for some reason you're no longer going to care for them. Usually an owner of a recreational horse or pet tries to find a home for the horse because otherwise the poor thing finishes up as pet food and sometimes for human consumption overseas. If a horse isn't valuable enough to not go into pet food, then giving the horse away for free to act as a companion horse for a person or another horse is a good option. Call me soft-headed and overly sentimental if you like, but the idea of a pet being sold by the kilo to be processed into food doesn't sit well with me.

But, it's a cruel world (especially for animals), and I understand that better than most because throughout my life, somewhere in my family there has been a farm or two. As it stands currently, my father-in-law breeds cattle and thoroughbred horses, but he's never sent a horse to the knackery. He goes out of his way to find genuine homes for his horses, whether it be for eventing, trail riding or as simple companions.

In my mind, good people do things not because they have to, but rather because they know they should. Sometimes you owe people something of yourself and sometimes you might need to fulfil a perceived responsibility. For me, good people do things they don't want to do because they know it is the right thing to do. For the most part, good people don't need 'the right thing to do' to be explained to them. I mustn't leave out those who mostly do things for show and politicians often fall into that category – in fact pollies just about own that category.

Prior to the 1998 federal election, one of our candidates was killed in an accident. The lady in question was the exact opposite of the way One Nation members and candidates were portrayed by the media and our other opponents. She was a happily married mother, successful businesswoman and piloted her own plane. Not a redneck or a gun owner or someone angry with the world because their job had been taken by an overseas buyer snapping up the Australian company for which they worked. Not some racist. This lady was a dream candidate for any political party: smart, well educated, successful, articulate and well presented. Sadly, she was killed by a terrible stroke of bad luck. While piloting her plane, she was forced to make an emergency landing. Her aircraft hit an obscured object, flipped upside down and burst into flames. Unable to escape in time, she burned to death while hanging upside down.

Where do I begin? Pauline didn't want to go to the funeral? She wasn't busy – she was just pottering about at home. Nothing was preventing her except her own brand of 'can't be bothered and couldn't give a toss'.

Nothing I could say would move her to going, not even the expectations of all the One Nation people who'd be there mattered to her. Doing it for show didn't count for Pauline either. In the end, I did manage to get her on her way, but she only went because I was more than clear that I was so upset with her that she couldn't see the need to be there, let alone the decency aspect that should have been apparent.

When she turned up at the funeral she was greeted as a returning hero. Many said how amazing it was that Pauline would take the time out from her busy schedule to attend.

Yes, 'busy schedule', now there's a joke. Pauline didn't have a busy schedule. Getting her to fulfil any reasonable responsibility was always like pulling teeth. As noted, on the day of that funeral she was just hanging around at home. Because Pauline was a federal member of parliament and the leader of One Nation, everyone except those closest, assumed she was flat-out on the run 24/7; and she should have been, but not so. I took particular note for myself of one twelve-month period during our time together in the party where, weekends aside, Pauline Hanson had more holidays and days off than anyone I've ever known. Great work if you can get it.

You see Pauline wasn't accountable to anyone. Everything was done for her and we covered up all the time she wasn't around. In reality, she only had to be in Canberra on parliamentary sitting days and had no other function apart from being a figurehead.

But the ordinary members and supporters thought she was flitting about everywhere trying to save Australia. I needed a whip and a chair to get her on any kind of tour or off to any of the meetings she needed to address.

There are lots of further examples of what a few of us saw of Pauline as she was day to day; what she got up to and her thoughts and treatment of people, but there are only so many pages.

It is worth however giving an insight into Pauline's approach to the formulation of policy. Though typical of how she thinks rather than an isolated example, one standout experience I had with her is worthy of retelling as it is both sad in the sense of disappointing, but also strangely hilarious in the sense of displaying her thinking, or not thinking, depending on how you look at things.

It was January 1998 and we knew a state election was going to happen relatively soon in Queensland, so a handful of us, including

Pauline, closeted ourselves in a house in the Gold Coast hinterland. There we were, the 'brains trust' (excuse me while I snicker at the thought of our collective intellect) of Pauline Hanson's One Nation, our thinking caps on, determining policy positions for the state election.

On this occasion, Pauline's contribution was, and I quote, 'I want to put up the aged pension by 10 per cent.' It's a nice thought, would certainly be popular and a real vote winner, no question, but where to begin when it comes to explaining to Pauline that it can't be done?

To start with, it's a state election and the aged pension is a federal responsibility, so it's simply out of the jurisdiction of the state government and utterly unrelated to state government policy. That's also where the discussion would normally end, but no, not when it's Pauline's idea. She wouldn't let it go. It didn't matter how I explained it, there was no making her see that it couldn't be done. I foolishly even attempted to explain that even if there was the capacity for such a policy, there was no way for us to credibly demonstrate how it would be funded.

As inconceivable as it is, in the end, the only way I could get her off this lunacy was to suggest I'd formulate a special Queensland state-based additional pension to top up the federal aged pension by 10 per cent, and that would be our policy for the coming state election. I did this with the expectation that by the next day she would have forgotten about it and that would be where it would end. Indeed, that is what happened. This was repeated on numerous occasions: she would come up with something that was effectively impossible and I would get it out of the way by suggesting a way of making it happen, knowing she'd quickly forget about it.

Ah, policy making with Pauline – well now you know!

Did Pauline and I have an affair? I only raise it because it's expected. Frankly, the notion of it merely detracts from what is important. The answer is no – there was no affair because if the allegations of antics between Pauline and me are correct, the timing of those allegations is several years before I met my wife, Lisa. It's unfortunate that over the years the story became one of me being unfaithful, when in fact the schedule of the gossip clearly places the supposed liaisons years before I met my wife-to-be.

Did anything physical happen between Pauline and me? You know the answer – you've already made up your mind, one way or the other. These days I no longer bother denying it, not because I acknowledge anything happened, but because I just don't care, and I'm comfortable for people to think whatever they like. After all, of what serious consequence is it anyway? The matter only rates a mention so I can't be accused of leaving it out.

Conclusion and regrets

I've agonised for a long time on behalf of people who believe Pauline will achieve something for them. It saddens me immensely that they too will go to their graves disappointed. But will they? I'm no longer sure. Perhaps just the fact that Pauline exists is enough for those who admire her? Maybe they will never really tally the successes, but be satisfied in their belief that Pauline is working for them and that somehow Pauline will save Australia? Like I noted earlier, she exists in their minds in a certain way, and maybe she always will.

It will always be a matter of mixed emotions for me. I care very much about Pauline's supporters, though many of them would blame me for all manner of things and hate me as a consequence. I feel responsible for them. I know I was the driving force in building this false hope, but I didn't build it to be false – against my will, that's just how it turned out.

There have been quite a few over the years who stuck with Pauline through so very much and yet she's lost many of them too. They were often the ones who knew her well and saw a lot of her. Sometimes they were people who opened their homes to Pauline when she was travelling and looking for a place to stay. Often they were people who had given Pauline a lot of money. They just kept the candle alight, despite growing suspicions that she wasn't what they thought. Some have contacted me and the conversation was always the same. It always started like this: 'I'm so sorry David, we didn't see it, we believed what was said. We believed what was said about you. Now we know the truth and it's too late.' Give or take a few words, that was always the sentiment of those calls.

Even today, with all I know of Pauline, my biggest regret is that I'm sorry I didn't make her succeed. Neither of us will change, and sadly, I understand my misguided hope of saving Australia was over before it even started.

Just as I don't know when I realised there was no more I could do, equally, I don't know when, if ever, I will entirely come to terms with that being the end.

My Time as a Broadcaster

I met David Oldfield through his work in the Liberal party back in 1993 and watched his time in politics unfold from there.

When David came to 2GB as a summer host at the end of 2007, many of my listeners made it clear to me they enjoyed his time on air. He seemed a natural for talk radio.

When an unexpected resignation made a full-time role available, I urged management to hire David to take the slot. David's Father had just died and he initially said no to the offer, but I advised him to take the job, and he did.

David has strong beliefs and he always stands up for what he believes. He is not afraid to take hits and he is not backward in his willingness to argue with those he considers to be wrong.

He is knowledgeable and demonstrates a clear understanding of the issues. He enjoyed sparring with callers and hearing their views, but he always allowed those with whom he disagreed plenty of time to have their say.

I am sorry David did not continue on radio, I believe he had a lot more to contribute.

– Alan Jones AO,
March 2018

I'd been interviewed many times on live radio all over Australia and I absolutely loved the immediacy of it. People were listening right then and there, and they could jump on the phone straight away to have their say. Radio as a career was certainly on my radar, but how does one break into radio? Usually you start at a little station somewhere and spend time getting known and building a reputation.

I couldn't really do that, given my marriage, concern for my elderly parents and living situation in general, there was no realistic way of moving from Sydney to a rural or regional radio station. I was already known publicly, so that would help, but still, it's a very hard job market to crack.

At that time, I could only go to either 2UE or 2GB. The ABC was out of the question; there was no way I could toe the party line there. You didn't know there was a party line at the ABC? Where have you been?

Looking at it, there are only so many shifts in a day, so between the two stations, there were only about twelve full-time gigs. It was almost like someone had to die for anyone new to get a chance, and goodness, the line of wannabes looking for a go is endless. Typically, radio broadcasters come from a journalistic background, so that counted me out, but the most successful people in radio in Sydney didn't list 'journalist' in their CV, so that helped count me back in!

It seemed to me the only chance I had was to get on air somehow and get heard by someone making decisions, and when I was contacted and offered a weekly guest spot on 2UE, I thought, here's a chance.

One day in mid 2007, I was driving along and got a call from a fellow I knew from Sydney radio station 2GB. He'd been listening to the occasional guest appearances I was making on their rival station, 2UE.

He said to me, 'David, you know, you get radio, you just get it.' He said that the program director at 2GB had been listening to me on the other station and wanted to talk to me.

The program director was a gentleman named John Brennan. I didn't know of John as such, but it wasn't long before I found out the person who wanted me to give them a call was considered the father of news-talk radio in Australia. John Brennan was a living legend in broadcasting. He had done it all. From the days of top-forty music, John Brennan had taken every radio station he'd programmed to number one.

In the news-talk format (talkback) he'd made 2UE number one, but he left to program 2GB and 2UE's loss was very much 2GB's gain. Just like when John was at 2UE, Alan Jones was now the breakfast host at 2GB. The powerhouse combination of the draw of Alan Jones and the programming skills of John Brennan stepped over 2UE and made 2GB Sydney's top station.

I wanted to break into radio and Australia's greatest programmer, from Sydney's number-one station, wanted to talk to me. Does it get any better than that?

I rang John and he had me come and see him. He got to know me, asked me lots of questions, and over a couple of weeks put me through three auditions. These were recorded with me giving short presentations on news topics and then taking mock calls. Each was like a mini show of thirty to forty-five minutes. John coaxed and coached and taught me all the way through the three auditions. At the end of each, he would listen to the tapes and give me a long, detailed written analysis of everything I got right, got wrong and all I must do to get better. All this led to me being contracted to do a long summer fill-in on overnights during the extended absence of the regular host.

Talkback radio is exactly that, lots of talk – there is no music. Playing a song was considered a weakness, a crutch used by those who ran out of things to say. It was a great job for someone with a lot to say – that would be me.

I started at midnight and talked all the way through the night till 5 am. It was gruelling, not only having to be awake all night, but on top of things, expressing views that had to stand up under the heavy-duty scrutiny of people whose lives included being plugged into radio all through the night.

Peter Brennan, the son of the legend, stayed with me to see me through my first night. His coaching, just like that of his dad, gave me what I needed to do the job.

Fortunately, I'd always been something of a night owl, but I wouldn't pretend it was ever easy. It was hard, but I loved every tiring moment of being able to say something live to thousands of people and then have them on the phone agreeing or arguing, putting their own spin on things. I'm not much for small talk, but get me going on something that matters and I can talk for hours; which was good, because that's what I had to do.

There were breaks for advertisements and the formal news, but the rest of the time it was just the callers and me.

If there was ever a song to play it would be a snippet in relation to something relevant on the day like the anniversary of the death of Elvis or maybe the opening night of a huge film. You never played the whole song, just a bit – usually the end bit so it didn't appear you were cutting it short.

It was an amazing time. I miss it now as I write about it and think back to what it was like, but life away from the microphone for an overnight host is virtually non-existent. One is essentially jetlagged the whole time. You live in a different world, as a night-time shift worker does.

I like to discuss, to debate, to argue and to uphold facts and logic in the face of nonsense, so it worked well for me, but gee I was tired. I remember an old radio veteran saying of the overnight shift, 'When you're not on air, you're never fully awake and never fully asleep, you're always somewhere in between.'

It's likely hard to believe, but I'm extraordinarily sentimental; I'm really very emotional in the sense of how my heart can be pulled apart by certain things, and I'm not backward in sharing my feelings. I remember one night in particular, shortly after my dad had passed away, reading out a letter I had written and becoming choked up.

> One of the hardest aspects of being a great broadcaster is to be natural. I vividly remember hearing David during his overnight show on 2GB – he was choked up and highly emotional. His father had just passed away and David was reading out a letter he had written, thanking his father for making him the man he was. It was compelling, captivating, brave and above all else natural.
>
> David understands better than most that broadcasting is a highly intimate form of communication and that words are more than just mere sounds – they can inspire, entertain, inform, or in my case, make you sob uncontrollably on the side of Parramatta Road.
>
> – Bruno Bouchet,
> executive producer, The Kyle and Jackie O show,
> Sydney's highest rating FM breakfast program, December 2017

Then, it came to an end, or seemingly so, as summer was over and the full-time host was returning. As quickly as it started, my radio career was over, when out of the blue, the regular overnight host just up and quit. Peter Brennan (John's son), who had by then become the program director at 2GB told me he went in to tell Alan Jones what had happened.

As Peter tells it, after getting the news that the person on the program that led into Alan's number-one breakfast show had resigned, Alan looked up from his desk with a very serious demeanour and merely said, 'Better get David Oldfield then.'

I was in a bad place as all this was happening and initially said no; timely and good advice from Alan Jones made me see sense. So it was that suddenly I had a two-year contract and a full-time gig on Sydney's number-one station.

I was auditioned by the best, ultimately, became his student and quickly became a full-time broadcaster. I know now that others looked on and wondered why I was being so personally groomed. For some, it was wrong that I hadn't started as a twenty-year-old at an outback radio station and slowly worked my way to the big city.

Towards the end of my contract, I got the chance to fill in on the latenight shift, 9 pm till midnight, as well as three weeks in the drive slot, 3–6 pm, through the summer of 2009–10.

On 20 January 2010, Group Program Director, Ian Holland, wrote to me – not just an email, but formally on letterhead.

> As we move back into survey mode and the regular 2GB team returns to the air, I would like to take this opportunity to thank you for the outstanding contribution you made to 2GB programming across the summer break.
>
> You have demonstrated clearly that you have the ability to present a more structured and evenly paced program. We were all most impressed by what we heard both on drive and on late nights.
>
> Your contribution added greatly to the success of 2GB over summer.

There I was, out of politics and two years into an entirely new career, and by all accounts that seemed to matter, I was doing a good job.

I'd found where I wanted to be, and I was grateful to have been so fortunate.

Then, within weeks, it started to become evident there were plans afoot to not renew my contract. How could that be? Why would that be? I'd been consistently praised by management and I'd hit record survey highs of 32.5 per cent.

There were fifteen stations in the Sydney radio ratings survey and a third of people who tuned in to overnight radio chose to listen to me. The feedback to the station was also excellent and a lot of listeners went out of their way make their positive feelings about me known. Some were even phoning and emailing other broadcasters at the station to tell them how much they loved my program; perhaps in some respects that didn't help?

As someone said to me later on, 'They weren't worried you would fail, they were concerned you would succeed.'

I was in Perth for the weekend at a friend's wedding when I got the phone call. It was short and not so sweet. Essentially, I got the DCM (Don't Come Monday), but I never got a reason why.

It is quite common in the media to suddenly just disappear under these circumstances. The station doesn't want to give you the chance to tell your audience what has happened. When you simply finish on a Friday and don't return, the station can say whatever they like. There was quite a backlash, people were unhappy, and they made that known to the station.

Even Alan Jones, the number-one broadcaster in Australia, was publicly clear in telling management that removing me was a mistake. Listeners had contacted Alan for help and he was very supportive. Some forwarded the relevant correspondence to me. To this day, Alan has always been eminently decent to me. He's a very good man, and a man of his word.

It's appropriate I note that while I was removed from the airwaves of 2GB without an opportunity to farewell my audience, the station appropriately fulfilled their contractual obligations, and were diligent in doing so. In that, I have no complaint.

It seems a long time ago and it's fair to say I was disappointed how my leaving 2GB came about, but within days, rival station 2UE was on the phone talking about getting me back on air.

Few commentators have generated the admiration and rapport with the listening public as David Oldfield did in his time at 2GB.

I am so privileged to know David Oldfield and to have worked with one of the best, who had an unparalleled feat of consistency (straight out of the Nielsen survey book for Sydney) being number one in the midnight till dawn show on 2GB and setting records at the time.

When I first met David, I was struck by his young demeanour, his exquisite courtesy, and his rock-solid faith in his own ability to be an outright success in talk radio. He had the right to be proud of his previous successes, yet I was stunned by his striking modesty.

He wore his thoughts about anything and everything on his sleeve. I looked at him in admiration. He deserved success because he prepared and flawlessly executed the content of each show. Not many do that in talk radio.

We met – I was impressed – and I rushed him into radio convinced he would succeed. I knew the overnight show would be in the hands of a warm, forgiving, non-judgmental and generous man named David Oldfield.

He was a serious customer most of the time but our meetings together (air-checking his latest show and pointing out his gems and things that had to be eliminated) were met with his unmatched and prodigious curiosity. At the finish of an honest but tough critique session he would always be filled with joy knowing his show that morning was spot on or could be much better with more selected content.

I taught him that content was king in talk radio. He learnt things quickly. He'd wander through the station hoping fellow hosts would give their opinion about his program. He was always flattered and deeply honoured that they obliged.

He was a terrific host for he knew and felt that talk-radio success is driven by talent that attracts loyal listeners day in and day out. He understood better than many that he had to be dynamic on air, engaging, and one who is genuine.

He was perfectly comfortable slicing himself open every morning and exposing his heart and guts every time he opened his microphone. He wasn't afraid to open up and share his opinions, feelings, hopes and fears while still being able to inform the audience about the subjects that affected their lives. He got it, he really did. He had the ability to inform and the talent to entertain.

I found David likeable, self-deprecating, witty, very intelligent and capable of saying things that you would like to say – but couldn't.

One of his greatest assets was being a storyteller. He always had a style of storytelling, with his editorials always taking you somewhere. He had the audience with him on every journey and together they arrived at the destination he had in mind. Each time he'd trot out a story I'd stop and listen for his unique observations.

He was driven to succeed, truly likeable, loveable and human. His wife Lisa and their two sons complete a fine Australian family.

He had the deadliest enemies. David had the very worst interpretations put upon his very kindest actions. They also slammed him by falsely reporting things he proudly put up. They tried to magnify or minimise his words. He was viewed with suspicion and condemnation. It was shocking – every day someone would try and slight him, even laughed to scorn when he gave of his very best on or off air. I regarded them (and told them so) as detestable, they were failures, casualties in radio and all they had were dysfunctional sideshows.

To this day I haven't a clue as to why David Oldfield was plotted against and vindictively disliked … even hated somewhat. I've thought long and hard about this fact and the only thing I can come up with is complete and outright jealousy.

It disgusted me so much it was one of the reasons I retired. My son Peter took over as program director and certainly took David to another level and a more attractive and important daytime shift.

Why was he so successful? He paid never-ending attention to the fundamentals and nailed the basics.

– John Brennan OAM,
program director, Australian radio legend, father of Australian talkback radio

Within weeks of my contract ending at 2GB, I was on air filling in at 2UE. They started using me to fill in for whoever was away, so I did stints in different shifts, but never again in overnights – my sleepless experiences and days of being one of the walking dead were thankfully over.

As summer of 2010 approached I was contracted by 2UE to take over the morning program, 9 am till noon. It was a great time. I loved that shift and I was now awaking at 5 am, rather than going to bed at 6 am as I did on the overnight shift.

Not only did I have more of a life again, but I also now had a son. Henry Ernest Oldfield had been born on 28 August 2010 and things really were coming up roses. I was doing the job I loved, had the shift I wanted, and I was a dad. Being a dad was the most important part of all, but combined with radio, it put me in a place where I thought I'd finally found what I should be doing with my life. I was middle-aged at the time, so it had clearly been a long road.

Not long after I started at 2UE, Peter Brennan was appointed program director. He had his dad's talents and a sound contemporary feel for radio. Peter knew radio. You would say he had 'an ear for radio'. He'd been a broadcaster and worked his whole life in the media. He was a credit to his dad and I often thought he should have stayed an on-air talent, but he chose programming – I guess it was in his blood.

Peter, just like his dad, was a great mentor. He continued where his dad left off and he taught me many things. I was always encouraged by his lessons and debriefings, and just like his dad, he's a truly great bloke as well.

I stayed in the morning shift until the middle of 2012 and then suggested to management that I be moved to nights, 8 pm till midnight. That probably seems strange, but I had previously renegotiated my contract to go to nights, however the station had trouble working out who would replace me. For a while, I was essentially contracted as the nights guy, but still doing the morning show. The time came when I thought it a good idea to formalise the arrangement and so I encouraged the move to nights.

In that shift, I had the most extraordinary producer. Indeed, one of my greatest regrets in ultimately leaving radio was losing Anthony Priwer. Anthony had the capacity to be an all-rounder in radio. There probably wasn't a job in any form of production or broadcasting that he couldn't do and not just do, but execute with an admirable level of expertise. He helped make my night program at 2UE and I remain enormously respectful of his diverse talents. He went on to work as a producer at Channel Seven and I hope they appreciate their good fortune in having him.

Working at 2UE became increasingly difficult. I didn't fit the way the station saw itself and it was clear I wasn't going to make much more of a go of things there. Peter Brennan departing the station compounded all that was wrong and with Peter gone, my producer Anthony and my audience seemed the only people left who appreciated what I was doing.

I was also concerned at what I thought would be devastating changes to the on-air line-up as I pictured who that would be in 2013. Another factor was that I'd recently become a dad for the second time, with the birth of Albert Theodore Oldfield on 5 July 2012. Albert had issues (that I discuss in detail elsewhere), so I needed to focus on him. As if that wasn't enough, my dear beloved mother was headed towards her end, and did in fact leave us in December of 2013.

I was contracted well into 2013, so I went to management to discuss the varying issues and I was able to negotiate an early release, which allowed me to finish at the end of 2012.

I was now free to care for my little sons, Albert especially, and to spend more time with my mum, and as it turned out, my expectations for the station in the coming year, came to fruition and it all went, as they say 'to hell in a handbasket', so I was pleased not to have been a part of that.

It's appropriate for me to acknowledge 2UE management, in particular, Chris Parker, acted in the most decent and professional manner with regard to my departure from the station. Apart from amicably releasing a joint statement, the contents of which were reported across the media, management allowed me to finalise my affairs at the station and say my farewells on air to my audience. It was the right way to go.

I miss radio. It remains my all-time favourite job.

David Oldfield enjoyed a successful albeit relatively short career as a talkback radio host on both 2GB and 2UE.

David possesses an extraordinary intellect. His knowledge and understanding of most things is exceptional. This combined with his wide life experience and well thought opinions on the issues that really matter equipped David to become a consummate talk radio presenter.

At 2GB David surpassed all expectations while hosting the overnight program. He steered the ratings to a record high of 32.5 per cent share of the listening audience.

And at 2UE, despite constant opposition and meddling by the incumbent Fairfax management, he achieved ratings double those who ultimately followed him while anchoring the Morning program. And when David was shifted to the Evening shift he consistently rated twice the station average.

David endured vicious and hurtful campaigns led by a handful of insiders at radio 2GB. And also while at 2UE, along with influential insiders at the troubled *Sydney Morning Herald*. These mostly left-leaning operatives ultimately caused David to resign his posts. But at *no* time did David ever resort to the systemic bullying, leaking of ill-truths to other media organisations, nor corrosive corridor conversations. David maintained his dignity and behaved in a manner that can only be described as thoroughly professional. And in a manner that always placed the radio station first.

– Peter Brennan,
former program director, radio 2GB and 2UE
and former New South Wales local content manager ABC Radio,
March 2018

Parenthood: Being David the Dad

Here are some thoughts that'll get me in trouble, though they shouldn't, but isn't that how my life has always been. I take responsibility for a lot of that impact by the way – should have kept my mouth shut!

I was a late starter as a dad and indeed, being an older dad seems to run in my family. My dad was forty when I was born. My grandfather was forty when my dad was born and my great-grandfather was forty when my grandfather was born. Not a lot of people my age have a grandfather born in 1878. I have eclipsed the family records however by being fifty-two when my first son was born and fifty-four when my second son was born.

Anyway, it is essentially correct that the age of the female is biologically more of an impediment to having children than the age of the male. Sure, medical science has stepped in and dramatically increased the potential age for motherhood, but that aside, the facts are clear. The great actors Tony Randall and Anthony Quinn were examples of very old dads – Quinn had his last child at eight-one and Randall waited till seventy-six to have his first and then another at seventy-eight.

I was once having lunch with the Kenyan High Commissioner and getting along very well as we exchanged stories when we started to talk about our families and he told me his dad was 104 – amazing!

He then went on to tell me his youngest sibling, a brother, was twenty-three – quickly doing the maths I said, 'That means your dad was eighty-one when he had your brother,' and then shot him my most quizzical look, to which he responded, 'Of course my father is a polygamist, so this was with his youngest wife, not my mother.'

Don't get me wrong, while the capacity to father a child stays with a man virtually to the end, I fully support the case of dads having a use by date. Surely that is in the interests of the children; that's my view anyway.

A dad has to be around for their children. Understandably there are difficult circumstances that often remove or semi-remove dads from their kids, but making babies when in your late seventies or early eighties isn't what a sensible person would consider part of a long-term plan. And that's how it turned out for Mr Quinn and Mr Randall. When Quinn died, his last child was five and when Randall died, his children were six and eight.

Children need their parents to be alive and kicking, not bringing them into the world when they are themselves only a few years away from a nursing home and a funeral service.

There have been times when I've been concerned about the age gap between my boys and me. I think gee whiz (I actually uttered other words entirely, but I'm avoiding swearing), when my youngest, Albert turns twenty-one, I'll be seventy-five!

The good news is I'm physically better off than my dad was at the same age, though I suspect he was more at peace mentally than I am, but again, I digress. I'm pretty active for my age. Actually, I'm pretty active compared to a lot of dads much younger than me. I have horses and I'm an active rider, galloper in fact – probably kill myself doing that at some stage! I've gotten my eldest into riding and we do that together at times, though he's only seven, so it's a bit limited, but I expect it to evolve into a great father and son activity as he safely becomes more competent. Henry has been riding for two years and his little brother, Albert, has just started having lessons. In the next few years, when they're ready, I hope to take them on a ride over the Snowy Mountains – horse riding and camping at its finest.

I also do a lot of strenuous bushwalking with my sons and I help out here and there coaching their Rugby team. A while back I built them an eleven-station military-style obstacle course to help with their core strength development while having tons of fun at the same time. I run fast, I jump, I climb, I lift heavy things, I can even snow ski better than most. I carry an array of injuries from various incidents, but fundamentally, I'm strong. I don't feel sixty – well most of the time I don't feel sixty!

What I'm trying to say here is, barring unforeseen cancer or other serious illness, I expect to be physically active for a long time to come. I have to be – I have these two wonderful strong little boys and they need me to do the things a dad should do, not the things a grandad should do.

As you may have picked up, I strongly take the view that included in all the responsibilities attached to being a dad, is the simple requirement of being physically able to give your kids what they deserve and require. A dad should be able to run with his children, to jump with them, to pass them a ball and to sink a few baskets on the court. In my view Tony Randall, at seventy-six, waited too long to have children. His, was an enormously selfish act in that in the end, after bringing them into the world, he deserted them. Too harsh? He couldn't help dying you might be saying and you're right, but at seventy-six, one must know they're not going to be around long for their kids, so having them then is just plain selfish.

Here's the thing – children change everything! My apologies if you know children change everything, but sadly, a lot of people seem not to get that. Indeed, quite a few people act as if children are accessory items in their lives.

Without seeming clichéd, I'm of the view that parenting must draw from you the highest level of commitment you'll ever make in your life. Not because of the bullshit about 'they're the next generation', and all associated rubbish, but rather, because you brought them into the world. You owe them; they only live because of you and they have a right to your best!

What I say now might piss you off at the start – if it pisses you off at the end, then you're a ratbag moron not deserving of oxygen and on that I absolutely mean to convey judgement at 100 per cent. Bringing a child into the world is about the most selfish thing anyone can do.

Yes, I did say it's selfish – selfish in the extreme, just in case someone missed it.

I meet quite a few people who delude themselves into the notion that their decision to have children has something to do with an opportunity for the child. There is no waiting room in the sky that serves as some kind of other-worldly orphanage where children wait in the hope a family might choose them. If it really is about an opportunity for the child, if you really do believe that, then adopt an already existing child who really will benefit from being taken from welfare into a family setting. If you won't do that, then admit that it really is about you, not the child.

I've known a few women who by choice became single mothers. In the cases I'm personally familiar with, it was never in the child's interest for that to happen; not because single mothers can't do a good job, again, it comes down to intent. And the intent I saw on those occasions was always a matter of creating a companion. Bringing into the world someone who will always love them, someone who really can't move on from them, as happened in the relationships that caused them to go down the path of single parenthood. This one won't get away!

I don't think there is anything wrong with wanting a child – clearly, I wanted children, otherwise, I wouldn't have them. I think it's unhealthy to delude oneself into thinking you're doing anything for a child by bringing it into the world. The only person you're doing this for, is you. There may be the exception to a degree that you aren't all that fussed on children, but you're going along with it for the sake of your husband or wife or so on, who desperately want children. If that's the case, as long as you're aware of the magnitude of the sacrifice you're making and willing to stick it out essentially for the rest of your life, then good on you. You are the exception to the rule – you're not selfish at all.

I believe parents need to acknowledge they're having kids for themselves. I think in that, you're positioned to understand the depth of the commitment and responsibility you're taking on. This poor little babe didn't ask to be born, is completely helpless and defenceless and totally reliant on you in a fashion that can be a real slap in the face for a lot of first-timers!

So, here's the thing, while having a child is enormously selfish, once they're born, you need to do a 180-degree turn and become utterly selfless. The helpless bundle of joy you've brought into the world without their consent is now owed absolutely everything by you. If you're not willing to pay that debt, don't bring the poor defenceless little being into the world in the first place. You're not giving them a chance, they unwittingly stake everything on you. There are no returns; there is no going back. This is a commitment vastly beyond that puppy or pussycat you have or had. If you mess up, the kid suffers the most and they had no choice in being here!

Parenthood isn't for everybody – some people aren't cut out to be parents. I don't think I was a natural for the job. It is my deep sense of responsibility and subscription to what I've put to you above that has made the difference for me.

I don't recommend being a parent. Do not misinterpret that. I love my sons beyond anything else; there is nothing more important to me than my sons and I wouldn't choose not to have them. Knowing what I know, I would still choose to have my boys, no question, but I recognise being a parent is a very difficult job that is frustrating and tiring, so, like I said, I don't recommend it because if you're really going to give it the effort your children deserve, you'll find it very hard. Like I said, being a parent isn't for everyone – if you aren't willing to put your children first in every situation, don't have them.

Perhaps it gets easier as they get older, but only in the sense that they can wipe their own bottoms and clean their own teeth and get dressed without help. Gee what a difference getting to that stage makes. While there are those stages you'll reach where their capacity to cooperate and do little things for themselves will be a great help, I'm told there are other stages where new issues arise. My boys are still really young, so I'm not there yet, but apparently the teenage years may be a struggle, for them and you.

My being a dad has been unusual in that I've been super hands-on, very much in the fashion of what society stereotypes as a 'stay-at-home mum'.

When my first son, Henry, was twenty-six months and my youngest, Albert, was five months, it became apparent that the best option for our family was for me to become a stay-at-home dad. I negotiated an earlier than expected end to my contract and broadcasting career and essentially retired – perhaps not entirely the best for me, but it is what it is. Lisa, resumed her career and I took on full-time responsibility for our boys.

We were very fortunate in being able to arrange to do this and it really was the right decision to make, especially for Albert. Henry had always been a dream child – a parent's dream child that is, in the sense he did everything you'd hope he would. He slept up to twelve hours at a time and was just the easiest baby. He crawled when he was supposed to, walked when he was supposed to, talked probably a bit early, was speaking in sentences very early and was so easy to feed. Not at all fussy – dream child!

Albert, however, was the opposite. Sorry if you're reading this one day Bertie, but son, it wasn't your fault, it's just the way things work out, or don't work out. Albert was every parent's nightmare, and I mean that in the nicest possible way. I guess we were spoiled by Henry. Both Lisa and I thought it was easy, and with Henry, it was.

The first thing is the issue of sleep. If they don't sleep, you don't sleep. Albert (Bertie) would wake up like clockwork every thirty to forty minutes. He'd need a feed or a nappy change or just have a cry and that went on till he was about twenty months. The only way to cope was for me to move into the spare room and sleep with Bertie. This meant Lisa wouldn't be woken ten times a night and I was better able to take care of Bertie. For close to fifteen months I felt like I wasn't sleeping at all. A lot of the time I was zombie-like, some would say I still am. These days I joke about the fifteen months when I didn't sleep and how it aged me ten years!

So, there we were, Bertie and me in the same bed with a bunch of nappies and bottles of milk and spare dummies on the side table. Most mums have probably had this experience, though probably not for such a long time, but for a dad, it's unusual – especially month after month after month without a break.

It soon became clear there was something wrong with Bertie.

He wasn't at all like Henry (Harry), he was angry and irritable and while he walked at ten months and was remarkably agile, he wouldn't talk. He had issues. Like I was saying, if you're going to be a parent you need to realise it can be like this and if it is, you need to be committed. When the months and months of sleep deprivation kick in, you need to hold things together.

Bertie stayed angry, violent even, and wouldn't talk. It was like he just didn't want to talk. Here and there he would say a word, but only ever in context. I will never forget pushing my Woolworths (brand placement) trolley with Bertie in it, and out of the blue, he points and said 'carrots'.

It's like, my God, he spoke, and I'm saying, 'Bertie, Bertie, carrots, carrots', but nope, he wouldn't say it again. He'd look at me as if to say, 'I've already pointed to the carrots and said carrots – why would I say it again.'

And that's how he was. He would only say something relevant. He didn't start with the usual Mummy, or Daddy, he just said a word here and there and always in context. He clearly understood everything said to him and from an early age would follow complex instructions, but he wouldn't talk. He did a lot of things that made me sure he was intelligent, including demonstrating that he had a great memory – he always knew where he'd left everything – but he just wouldn't talk. He seemed to take everything in and, indeed, when he did speak, it was evident he'd learned what things were and committed their names to memory for his occasional use in context, but in no way could you entice him to speak.

And he was so angry. Sometimes he reminded me of mentally challenged children I'd helped years before. He seemed frustrated and I started to worry he might hurt himself like those mentally challenged children had.

He was on his way to being two years old and still not talking and I couldn't help but be concerned we'd brought an angry imbecile into the world. Yeah, I realise how terrible that sounds, but when there's something wrong with your child, you think all sorts of things, some of which other people without the same experiences would think of as pretty bad.

It's in me that when something isn't working, my mind goes ahead in leaps and bounds thinking through all the possible terrible results. It's never just about the here and now and the issues as they are, I extrapolate everything right out of the ballpark. For me, a problem immediately has long-term consequences, so I sometimes seem to over-respond to things. Note that I didn't say overreact. I'm pretty much conditioned to not react, but rather, respond. I very quickly think through situations and related ramifications and respond. For me, reactions are something to avoid.

To consider and then respond is mostly a good thing, but the problem is that when your mind races ahead laying down a path of consequences, the clarity of that can disturb you into coming to the worst possible conclusions. So for me, the possibility of my son perhaps being challenged in some way immediately hits me with thoughts including, I'm a really old dad, who will take care of him when I'm gone. It gives you a lot of, 'Oh fuck' moments all at once.

Mostly, if anyone gets an angry or aggressive response from me, it's because that's what I wanted them to get, rather than me just reacting. Okay, if I haven't already admitted it, I'll do it now, I'm an angry person largely kept in check by willpower! All the worse that makes it because I'm also thinking Bertie may be angry because of me; though my wife Lisa is pretty angry as well, oh, and she tends to react quite a bit, so maybe we're both to blame?

Next stop, my doctor for a referral and then to a paediatrician and that produced some of the worst times I've had as a father. The paediatrician started to talk about Fragile X. What's that you may very likely ask. I certainly did and the answer isn't something to go away with in your mind while forced to wait for test results. Fragile X Syndrome is a genetic disorder that causes intellectual disability and is said to be the most common of causes for inherited autism. Sufferers have trouble understanding and processing information, which in turn causes learning, development and behavioural issues. There are a host of other signs and symptoms, including delayed speech development and aggression – yep, that's Bert.

It's natural that you hope and pray this cannot be so – not my child, not my little boy, it's so unfair. It's not fair for anyone, but one tends not to be thinking about others in such moments. How could this be? And of course there's the guilt. What did I do? Was there something done wrong during his pregnancy? Is there anything like this in our families?

Despite what my critics think they know, I'm actually a very emotional person – hell, I'm a Cancer – but most of that is deep and offset by the strange fact that I'm also the opposite as well, in that I'm crazily pragmatic and rational.

Once I let the gamut of what the doctor was saying go right through me, my rational self kicked into gear, but goodness, when you're paying a specialist a lot of money to advise on your child's wellbeing, you expect the information to be something you must take seriously, so I did.

While the expertise of the advice meant I couldn't completely disregard the doctor's thoughts, I didn't ever really think Bert was mentally challenged, but clearly, I had to go through with everything the specialist recommended. He was angry, violent and he wouldn't speak, but he didn't have any other signs or symptoms that lined up; apart from that, he'd continually demonstrated intelligence and his talking issue seemed to have all the characteristics of choosing not to speak.

Still, there was the matter of hearing tests, blood tests, tests, tests and more tests – lots of tests and waiting and wondering. A very worrying time to which many parents would relate.

I realised at the time that my own thoughts on his condition might be an emotive response to try and convince myself he was really okay, because it was going to be something we could fix. It's such a natural thing to, against all the odds, believe things aren't as bleak as they appear, to invoke God through prayer and wish in every way you can that it'll all work out. I did that to a degree, but I'd also spent so much time with Bert that I just couldn't see his problems as being anything to do with his mental abilities or lack thereof. He'd consistently demonstrated intelligence.

When Henry was born, within hours he was in intensive care because his oxygen levels were dropping and seeming to run all over the place. Lisa was a mess. I understand that; she'd just given birth and was vulnerable. She'd barely had a chance to hold Henry and he was whisked away to intensive care and plugged into every conceivable machine. He was surrounded by very premature children, one of whom was also an Oldfield. None of them made it, despite the best of care.

Lisa thought she was going to lose Henry. How out of place he looked with all the tiny souls around him – some only weighed 800 grams and here was our Henry, full term, over 3 kilos and looking fit. But there go his oxygen levels again, and the machines don't lie – what's causing it?

Every time I'd study our little son's breathing, connected as he was to so many beeping machines, I'd think, the little bugger is holding his breath. Sure enough, he'd clearly hold his breath, the oxygen machine would freak out and then he'd breathe again, and all would return to normal. Over time, the result was a readout that demonstrated all these sudden and continual inexplicable drops of the oxygen level in his blood. They didn't seem so inexplicable to me. He was holding his breath, but you had to stand and carefully watch him for a while to work that through. The readout was absolutely correct, but it couldn't pick up he was apparently doing it intentionally.

Why does a baby only a few hours old hold their breath? I don't know, and it turned out neither did anyone else. Maybe because he can? Little troublemaker, yes, that's what it was. Henry spent five days in intensive care, had brain scans and every test available, and all along he was just holding his breath.

There was never anything wrong with Henry, but it was hard on Lisa. As his worried mum, she couldn't help but fear the worst, which was unusual for her because she's always been the 'glass is half full' kind of girl – it's me who is the negative 'glass is half empty' person.

When I looked for hours at Henry in his humidicrib I was convinced he'd be fine. Did I know something everyone else didn't? I have to take into account the unflinching belief I had that he is my son and he's strong and healthy, and it'll all be okay. Such are often the thoughts of people who refuse to accept the reality that there really is something wrong. Maybe that's all I was doing too; just failing to accept there is a problem that hasn't been determined?

Lisa was fearful Henry was going to die. I never thought that or even close to that for a second. Perhaps I was just balancing out Lisa's fear, which was unusual for me, because I'm the more likely pessimist. But when I looked into my little baby's eyes, I saw my dad – it was as if he had been reborn in my son. He looked so knowing and he seemed to have what would be called 'an old soul'. I'm not a person who believes in that stuff, but there it was.

Today, as I pen this so many years past those first few days with my little first born in intensive care, I picture his face and the look in his eyes as if I'm looking into them again now. He seemed comfortable and peaceful, wise even. A week after Henry was born, he and Lisa were home. Yep, he was just voluntarily holding his breath. There wasn't anything wrong with him at all, but gee he gave his mum a fright. We brought him home from the hospital knowing he'd had every test there was to have and passed them all. I took the view he'd probably be a diver like me because he had a natural propensity for breath holding!

Four years later and here I am with Bert. Different situation, but same problem – what's wrong with him? Ultimately something good came of all the tests – they showed there was nothing apparently wrong with Bert. No Fragile X and he wasn't challenged in any way, and while those terrible days and weeks of tests and awaiting results were behind us in the most positive way, he still wasn't talking.

Though there is no sign of it, I had a speech impediment as a child – it was rectified brilliantly by an amazing speech therapist named Katherine Blowen. How I would have loved Bert to go to Miss Blowen, but tragically, cancer had killed her. A great loss to all who knew her – a truly wonderful lady.

So here we have it, there appears to be nothing physically or mentally wrong with Bert and I'm just as frustrated as ever, but at the same time enormously relieved as I'm of the firm view we'll get through this.

Incidentally, I'm acutely aware that in these times, PC adherents are always offended. There will be those who are horrified at me describing Bert as having apparently nothing physically or mentally wrong with him. While there are those who get angry at terms such as disabled, or the expression, nothing physically or mentally wrong, and they prefer the idea of differently abled or differently challenged, I assure you, if you can't talk or walk or manage yourself like most, there is something wrong, and it is a terrible misfortune. That's not to say those with serious physical issues can't have amazing lives and make extraordinary contributions – some will achieve far more than lucky people who have the full function of every part of their body. Are they helped by referring to them in ways that suggest they are the same as lucky people? I don't think so, though I'd understand if they were in on the hoax as well, then perhaps it adds to their self-esteem and that may justify the ruse.

Words such as spastic and retard should cease to be a part of our language, if they haven't already, but I think to pretend things are much more positive than they are is a shaky path. Mind you, I understand if that's just me. There is a general desire to paint everything positively to the point of the ridiculous. I don't subscribe to that, though if it helps people better deal with their lives, then perhaps there is more good in it than bad.

Anyway, back to Bert. We're throwing everything at him, in an effort to get him talking and diminish his angry behaviour.

I found a great therapist for Bert and she started to get him a bit more interested in talking. She also noted his tremendous anger and, likely rightly, identified this as Bert expressing his frustration. With her advice we got in an occupational therapist, and together in joint sessions, they got to work helping Bert with his aggression and expression.

The news is full of stories of little kids with incurable diseases and we read of parents who are going through the hell of knowing their child probably won't see their fifth birthday. Parents who are told there is nothing more that can be done.

Some take every penny they have and spend it trying for cures all over the world, while others put their faith in God – a questionable approach at best, but for some, their faith will help them, and in every practical sense, that's a good thing. Many of those who ultimately lose their child will get through that mostly because they'll see it as God's will. Everything that befalls you or me should always be put in perspective, and so in that fashion, there were times I felt a bit pathetic in that I had a child who wouldn't speak, while others had a child who was going to die.

Once I was sure Albert wasn't mentally challenged, I occasionally felt like I should consider myself lucky he didn't have a lot more wrong with him – I should feel lucky I have him as he is and not much more afflicted or dying. It's a bit like that old tale of the man who felt sorry for himself because he had no shoes until he saw a man who had no feet – perspective! But as clear as the lesson is, it isn't always easy to be grateful that what is wrong with your child isn't as bad as the suffering of another. It's your child and you want them to be perfect and healthy and it's difficult not to feel wronged on their behalf.

The stories of what happens to others should slow us down. They should stop our minds racing and they should make us take stock of what we have, but while I can't get past loss, I still try hard to focus on what's good.

Precisely at the time I was writing about the experience of Bert, I received a text from someone I knew a long time ago. It was about their son. I've left out names and funeral details, but here's the rest of it:

'Sad that our son died of cancer. Oncologists gave up in August 2016. We tried alternative therapies which worked well for a while. I trust that you, Lisa and the kids are well and valuing each day.'

★★★★

Little Albert is still very angry, and he really is a handful who is easily turned to rage by his provocative older brother Henry – it's apparent they love each other deeply, but Henry really knows how to push his brother's buttons.

Henry and Albert will likely read this one day, so for them, I'll put that little boys can be cruel, probably little girls too, but I haven't raised girls so I won't go with that notion. My boys are demonstrably about as close as brothers could be – sometimes I would see them hug and look out for each other, and it warms my heart to know they have each other. Other times, quite often in fact, I have to separate them because they're so violent, they'll really seriously hurt each other and sometimes, they have hurt each other quite badly when I didn't get between them fast enough. That made it particularly tough when they were going through angry periods as I had to be very close by at all times. I couldn't leave them in the house while I mowed the lawn.

It worries me how violent they are toward each other – on one occasion Henry broke Albert's collarbone – Albert's same collarbone Henry broke in a trampoline accident two years before. This time around Henry said it was another accident, but as I explained to him, 'Son, when you roughly throw someone to the floor in a fight and their collarbone gets broken, that's not an accident!'

Something being an accident is a great excuse for us all when in fact there are few accidents really, but rather, a lot of stupid things done without consideration for the circumstances and likely consequences. A simple matter of the sequence of events that can be traced back to show the real reasons behind the 'accident', and hence that it wasn't an 'accident' at all.

My father was an enormously wise man with an extraordinarily high level of common sense and I'm fortunate that a lot of what he tried to teach me eventually made its way into my character and actions. However, a lot of those lessons were not learned early enough and some are yet to really take hold.

In a classic and terribly upsetting way, I continue to be angry with myself because I feel I didn't appreciate my dad enough while he was alive and, sadly, my own sons will probably do the same with me. If you've been fortunate enough to have great parents, then it seems only natural to draw on their lessons for use with your own children. I see more of my dad in me each day and if he is somehow watching, he'd be seeing it too.

My mum was a very loving and special mother, and it continues to hurt me when I think of the things I should have done for her and didn't. My dad's words ring in my head, 'I won't be here forever'. To which I used to say, 'Where are you going?'

And they do go, and no matter how old they are, it's always too soon. If you love your parents and they're good people, it's a terrible thing to lose them – for most people, it'll be the worst thing that will ever happen to them.

I don't want my sons to grow up angry and bad tempered like I did, and I'll beat it out of them if necessary – yeah, that was a joke. I have smacked my children and immediately regretted it – you cannot use violence to teach a person not to be violent! I'm certain violence merely serves to create fear and intimidation and bring about the desire for retribution. There is that saying, 'violence begets violence'.

When my sons go at each other, I try to explain by asking the question, 'Where does it end? Henry, if you punch Albert and he punches you back, then you kick him, and he grabs you in a chokehold, then where does it end?'

It can only end of course when someone decides to be the one who'll be the first to stop. Given supposed adults appear to have trouble taking that on board, imagine the difficulty conveying that message to my little sons.

I'm certain punishment needs to be much more considered – something that teaches the lesson that there are consequences for wrongful actions, but put into practice without aggression.

As I say that, parenting is enormously frustrating when children won't listen and when they do something you've just begged them not to do, and in particular, when they do things that are dangerous to themselves. There are times when it seems all you can do is smack. I've been through this argument with myself so many times and every time it ends badly with me chastising myself for being a bad dad.

What to do when you can't reason with someone? Get physical or walk away – those are the choices when dealing with adults, but you shouldn't get physical with your child and you mustn't ever walk away. You are responsible for their existence, you owe them everything! Of course when children are only a few years old, there's little to no success going to come from reasoning with them. Maybe the best course is to hug them tightly, tell them how much you love them and try as simply as possible to explain how much it will mean to you if they're good.

Yeah, I don't know, and I don't want you to get the idea I'm passing myself off as an expert on children because I'm not – I'm just a dad desperately trying to get it right and I beat myself up quite badly whenever I think I haven't done the job as well as they deserve.

Just before I started writing today, Albert was expelled from his swimming class. Albert, as I write this, is only five years old. He's a troublesome boy – he just won't do as he's asked, told or begged. As his mother says, 'He's so contrary.'

When I brought him home from swimming, I had a long talk with him and he promised to start being a good boy. Within ten minutes, he was doing the most angering and frustrating things and I said to him, 'What happened to being a good boy?' He said, 'I'll start on the next day.'

After Albert was expelled from swimming school, Lisa said to me, 'He'll either end up in jail or running a country.' Yep, that's our Bert and in fairness, he gets a lot of his personality from me, so yet again, my fault.

To you Albert, when you read this one day, understand Daddy has always loved you more than anything and I've always believed you would ultimately do amazing things – I mean amazing in a completely positive sense!

And on doing amazing things, when parents are asked about what they'd like their children to be when they grow up, you hear a lot of them say 'Whatever makes them happy.'

Yeah, I think that's nice, I want that for my sons too, but they need to be pushed to be in a position to do whatever makes them happy, which equates to them doing something they like. Again I say to you, they were brought into the world by you – they didn't ask to be here. You need to do a lot more than leave them to 'Whatever makes them happy.'

Another typical question to those who are about to be parents is, 'What are you having a boy or a girl?'

A lot respond with, 'We don't care as long as it's healthy.' Others give you, 'We don't know, we want it to be a surprise.' Surprises are for Christmas and birthdays, not the bringing into the world of a human being.

As for, 'We don't care as long as it's healthy,' I don't believe many who say that really feel that way, they're just being politically correct.

A lot of people clearly have a preferred gender in mind for their child. It's not uncommon for men to want boys and women to want girls. It's not always that way, but like I said, it's not uncommon. In fact, I'd put to you that it's very common, much more so than many would let on, but for a range of reasons they don't make it obvious.

At least for some this is because they don't want to have that discussion with their other half and that's understandable. I mean, how do you react if you really seriously want a boy and you get a girl. How do you take back what you said? You can picture the conversations in years to come: 'Your father never wanted a girl!' Or this one, 'How did you become such a tomboy? My daddy always wanted a boy.'

I don't want to leave out those prospective parents who deny gender actually exists as such, because they see it as a social construct and hence take the view their baby will determine its own gender when it's old enough to decide. To you people, I say put this book down, lock yourself in a room somewhere, rock yourselves gently in the corner and forget about ever breeding. Your thoughts on these matters are utterly without intelligence or any genuine rational considered thought.

Lisa and I didn't fit any of these categories and maybe you already picked that up – we were always both quite outspoken about wanting boys.

Shock horror, how would it have been if we'd had girls? Not a problem really, there are lots of people wanting to adopt healthy children … clearly a joke. We'd have loved girls just the same, but spent even more time worried about them.

Lisa's position was clear and in fact I checked it with her again as I was writing this. Me: 'Tell me again why you didn't want to have girls?' Lisa, 'I'd just be worried about them all the time.'

Me: 'Would you say it's come from being a girl that's made you think that way?' Lisa: 'Yes, probably.'

I'm of the view there is a bit of the God complex running through most people in that when it comes to children, their desire for a particular gender comes from wanting to create them in their own image.

I've known of couples where the mother so desperately wanted a daughter, that there was a genuine disappointment when there were three healthy boys in a row. In one particular case, I'm aware the family situation was very tense because the mother was filled with disappointment at not having a daughter. Her sons knew, and it affected them.

I suppose fathers have been in similar situations and also been disappointed they didn't have any sons. Depending on one's culture, it's devastating to not have sons. Interestingly, I'm not aware of any cultures where it's devastating to not have any daughters, but maybe they exist?

I side a bit with Lisa in that I also think boys are a bit easier, but much of the choice where I was concerned was about how much easier it would be for the child. What do I mean by that? Well, I take the view that the world is an easier place for men, except of course during the times they have to deal with women … another joke, or maybe not.

I think women get a bad deal in many aspects of life and I wouldn't by choice put someone through that. In saying that, I'm sure women can have just as satisfying lives as men. In many cases there will be women who will have better lives than many men, but generally, I think the deck is somewhat stacked against women.

You may be reading the above and thinking, perhaps even shouting, 'Why don't you do something to change the world to be a better place – a place into which you would happily bring a daughter?'

You might be asking, 'Instead of acknowledging that issue and trying to avoid it for your own family why not work to make the world better for everyone else's daughter?'

It's a good question. By and large, I've found people very hard to help. People are their own worst enemy, and in that, often it is the group that feels discriminated against, that causes much of the trouble for themselves. It is possible to help individuals and to even make a difference for little groups here and there, but not so much that it changes for the better the lot of an entire gender.

I also believe that when it comes to these matters 'each force is met with an equal and opposite force'. And in that I mean that what is a forward movement for one group becomes an equal backward movement for another.

Then there is the matter of culture. Many cultures are very anti-women and almost tolerate them only in roles seen as appropriate by the judgement of men. Those cultures are moving in on western society in a big way, but that's not so much about parenthood and best considered somewhere else.

I'm of the view the world will see its end before men and women sort out the issues between the sexes in a fashion that will meet the agenda of feminists, so frankly, my time is my time and I'll direct it where I see fit.

So, no daughters for me, and whether or not you can see why, it is what it is.

Apart from obvious matters like creating a safe environment for my children and making sure they're well-nourished in every respect, I see one of my main responsibilities as doing all I can to not pass on my own flaws, but rather to do all I can to make my children better than me in every way.

As far back as twenty years ago, I had a disagreement with a journalist because I said I wanted my children to be bigger, stronger, faster and smarter than me and I felt it was my responsibility to make that happen. Indeed, I consider this to be the responsibility of every parent. Seriously, why would we want each generation to just be the same as the one before? Surely we should work for those who follow us to be better?

I've made it clear the world is a difficult place and getting uglier day after day. If you don't see that and still imagine butterflies and teddy bears, then my boys will likely eat yours. And that will be the true natural order of things – survival of the fittest. The more western society strives to cultivate men with less and less masculinity, the more the strong will stand out, and the more the weak will one day need them.

Every day, I spend time training my boys' minds and bodies. I hope I'm preparing them to be able to deal with just about anything the world throws at them. That is my job, the most important job I've had. They horse ride, they play rugby and I've started them in the same style of karate I did as a youngster. At the appropriate time when they're older, they'll also learn proper safe use of various firearms, but hell, Henry is also learning piano – I mean we're not philistines! We're descended from Vikings though, so there's a chance they might sack a monastery or a village at some stage.

Call me old-fashioned if that's your thing, but there are aspects of gentlemanly behaviour that I teach my boys. The first, and one I repeat often, is that they never ever hit a female; however tempting for some it might be, I've always avoided it and I want my boys to do the same. In some respects, feminists should accept the right for a man to hit a woman if she has hit him, but for me, hitting a woman isn't something a man does. Sorry, but it's the fairer sex thing – one just doesn't hit.

Mind you, in one's own self-defence, if they get in too close, you may certainly restrain them from hitting you, and I've done that, but don't use undue force and don't use offence as a form of defence in this case. If a woman becomes violent, and that's a lot more common than society is willing to openly accept, then extricate yourself – just get away from them. That's what I teach my boys. Some women think men run from them because they're scared, but be assured, if it is ever my sons doing the running, it's not because they're scared, it's because their dad taught them not to hurt you.

Hitting other males you might ask? Well, I've made a point of teaching my sons to never hurt anything they don't have to hurt. I won't even let them kill an ant. So I don't want them in fights. I'll teach them to evade and escape. The satisfaction isn't worth the potential trouble. Besides, others weigh in with broken bottles or possibly knives. Depending on where you are these days, some grub may even have a gun. If that isn't enough, even winning a fight with relative ease usually leaves you with an element of injury because you can't be warmed up 24/7 and if you have time to stretch, you have more than enough time to leave!

All that said, that doesn't mean they won't be trained appropriately. I'm training them already, they just don't know why. If the time ever comes where there is no other option, they'll know what to do to defend themselves and others. That's no idle macho bullshit by the way. If you think we live in peaceful times where the capacity for physical action isn't a necessary skill, then you're in a dream state.

My sons are also being taught to say please and thank you, how to use cutlery and where to put their knife and fork on their plate when they're pausing and when they've finished eating.

Feminists will be upset when my sons open doors for them and invite them to go first and likely they'll be bewildered when my sons put down not just the toilet seat, but the lid as well. I hope they display good manners, know what to say and when not to speak at all – something I took too long to learn.

As soon as they could understand I started teaching them to look into a person's eyes when shaking their hand or when speaking to them or listening to what they're saying – don't look away.

I want them to tell the truth and to understand what my dad taught me, the only acceptable lie is one told to protect someone else. And to that last one, I'd add, they'll need to know how to avoid answering questions that people have no right to ask. There's more of that now than in my dad's day.

That's me being a dad. I may have left something out – it's on-the-job training and I'm learning every day. I have never taken a job so seriously as this job of being Henry and Albert's dad. It isn't something you can screw up and start over. You have to get it right and keep on track. As someone once said, failure is not an option.

Media and Reality TV

My presence in the media very much predates getting into politics. It's fair to say I'd had my fifteen minutes of fame, so to speak, through appearances on Donnie Sutherland's music program, *Sounds* and newspaper articles and TV stories on things I did while in the diving industry. That stepped up to a degree when I was elected to Manly Council in 1991. The local paper, *The Manly Daily*, was the most widely distributed and most read local newspaper in Australia. It came out five days a week and its influence locally back then was extraordinary.

As a councillor, or alderman, as the title was when I was elected the first time, and later as a Liberal candidate, I garnered a lot of local press and occasional pieces in the major metropolitan newspapers as well. Founding Pauline Hanson's One Nation and being Pauline and the party's principal advisor took all that very much to the next level. Over the next couple of years, I was the subject of major stories on all four TV channels, news and current affairs. Hard to imagine these days, but back then there were only four channels 2, 7, 9 and 10. The major newspapers all over the country, as well as magazines, carried stories about me, as did all the radio stations. There was a lot of interest and in many cases there was a considerable agenda in how the stories were carried – PHON was upsetting the applecart and the fault was mine.

In the middle of 1997, just months after the party was launched, Pauline was tired of the media and actually refused to do any more. Yes, you got that right, Pauline, the leader of what was rapidly becoming the third largest political party in Australia, decided she was finished with the media. Suffice to say, that decision was a disaster. It meant I was left the job of doing what she should have done. If I didn't do it then it wouldn't get done and PHON would have been left without a public profile.

There was no social media. To get to the people in 1997, you had to be on the news, and Pauline dug her heels in and went to ground. This meant it wasn't uncommon for me to be on the nightly prime time TV news on as many as three of the four channels, three to four nights a week and that went on for months.

The uninitiated think if their name is in the newspaper once or twice or perhaps a photograph, then they'll get some kind of profile, and goodness, if you get a chance to be on TV, then everyone will know you. The reality is it takes constant attention before people start recognising you in the street. I was getting that attention and my profile quickly reached the point where I couldn't go anywhere without being recognised. The unfortunate part of this for PHON was that while I was doing a good job and was largely unassailable when confronted by those who opposed us, most of these appearances should have been done by Pauline. However, as Pauline didn't want to do any more media – and for a long time there was no changing her mind – if I didn't do it, then the public would simply not have heard anything from PHON, only from those who were attacking us. Various troublemaking party members thought I was trying to steal the limelight, they just wouldn't get it in their heads that if I didn't do it, it didn't get done. They didn't want to believe Pauline was bunkered down and wasn't going anywhere near the media. It was another example of the issues I faced in the role I was in – damned for doing it, but if I hadn't, the party's public profile would have just disappeared.

It was a very unusual thing for Australian politics that I would be fronting the media representing the party on a range of matters, but around the world, especially in America, such a role as a spokesman is often the norm.

Some people are interested in fame for fame's sake and that is so much more the case these days, but for me it was all a matter of necessity. When I was in music, media was obviously important. When I had my business, I took any opportunity to promote that business and in politics, without the media, there was no way to get your message out. The craziness of being famous for the sake of being famous doesn't interest me, quite the contrary, but what fame can do to help you achieve things, is another matter and that was my only reason for ever being in the media.

As difficult as it may be to believe, I'm naturally shy. Even these days, I feel more comfortable talking to 1000 people about something I think matters than to a couple about nothing. I've never been much good at small talk, but if I've got something to say, I get up and I say it.

Apart from all the time spent being interviewed on TV, radio or for newspapers and magazines, I've so far done what amounts to five reality-style TV series. I say 'so far' because there may yet be more to come, though I'm not sure what's left. Perhaps Senior Citizen in Paradise or Elderly Widow Wants a Wife – those shows don't exist currently, but who knows?

Survivor

While I was still a parliamentarian in 2006, I got a call out of the blue from a producer about doing a show. He said, 'Have you heard of The Mole?' I said, 'Not really, but I've been out with a few.' My dark sense of humour has likely caused feminists to close my book at this point, if they hadn't already.

So there it was. Would I consider appearing in a reality TV show about a group of people trying to work out who the traitor was in their midst? It was suggested to me my political background made me a perfect candidate.

Perhaps that was true since politics is awash with treacherous people one has to manoeuvre on a daily basis, and of course I'd been accused of being a traitor as well, so perhaps someone from politics was a good choice.

As it turned out, once they were sure they had me committed, the program was revealed to be *Survivor*. Channel Nine had the rights to

Survivor, but Channel Seven had found a loophole in which they could do a 'celebrity' version.

Before I go any further, this would be a good time to look at who or what constitutes being a celebrity. Simply put, it's a famous person usually associated with sport or entertainment, or just anyone who is well known. I'm well known though at times I've been more well-known and other times less well-known, but I have never pictured myself as a celebrity.

To me, celebrities are really famous people with fame that is clearly on an international scale. Celebrity for me is like Brad Pitt, Sean Connery, Pink, Mick Jagger – you get the picture. None of those people, or anyone else who would fit my notion of celebrity, is ever going to do reality TV, so it's left to we lesser known people who perhaps have a reasonable local profile for something or other. Of course, there will always be people included in these programs who might have been well known a long time ago or aren't really well known at all, but can be vaguely passed off as having a profile.

As these shows move into a second or third series, it can get a lot harder to cast them and there is a tendency to get a few too many people of whom most viewers have never heard. All this leads to the allegation of various people not being celebrities, something which I agree with a lot of the time, especially so given I've already made it clear I don't see myself as a celebrity.

Also, somewhat interestingly, from what I've seen, a person might reasonably be well known and in that, fit the bill as a celebrity, but to someone who doesn't like them, or simply isn't a fan, they will not be seen that way. Yes, being liked or disliked makes a big difference to not only whether one is seen as a celebrity, but even as to whether one is deemed intelligent.

I've found, as perhaps have you, that most people very poorly evaluate people they don't like. Keep in mind they may not know the person other than seeing them on TV, but if they don't like them they have difficulty accepting anything positive about that person. For a lot of people, those they take a disliking to, or with whom they believe they have some disagreement, are rarely considered smart, let alone nice.

I'd call this 'disagreement from a distance'. It's where you haven't met a person or had any conversation with them, yet from something you've seen or heard of them, you've formed an opinion of them. On the other hand, it may be a matter of 'agreement from a distance', where you like someone you really know next to nothing about because they said something that resonated with you. In the case of true celebrities, one may have a very strong view one way or the other based on a character they played in a movie or because of a song they wrote or sang.

I've been guilty of these things myself, but since being a victim of it as well, I'm now a lot pickier about judging public figures I don't know.

What strange beings we are, so driven by emotions that make no practical sense. And how silly am I to put it that way – emotions rarely, if ever, make practical sense, though some are demonstrably more sustainable than others.

Like I said, the first show I did was *Survivor* – a celebrity version, but for all intents and purposes, it was probably about as gruelling as the non-celebrity version, though shorter, so less time under duress. The cast was the classic mix of those who were something, had been something, or hadn't been much at all but could be sort of portrayed as having celebrity of some kind. In fairness to the producers, finding people who can head off out of the country for a month and who are also people with some claim to fame is a challenge.

We had Guy Leech, a world champion iron man, Wayne Gardner, a world champion motorcycle rider and Elton Flatley, who had recently been vice-captain of the Wallabies. Then there were the bikini models, actors, dancers, a self-proclaimed witch and Amber Petty, who was billed as the royal bridesmaid, as she was a close friend of Mary, Princess of Denmark. Last but not least was Ben Wynn, who had no celebrity, but was a survival expert and the prize in a particular challenge; he would join the tribe who won that challenge and be a huge asset in the hunt for food.

It may seem strange, but for me, Ben was the real celebrity. He was a former member of the Special Air Service Regiment (SASR) and a combat veteran. He had credentials that I truly admire. He'd done things I never had and never will, so he was the standout for me.

Guy Leech was without doubt the fittest person I'd met and even though he was forty-two at the time of filming, he had endurance that was easy to respect. Wayne Gardner had been the very best in the world in his field and such achievements must always be seen as significant. I thought Amber was genuinely nice, I liked Elton, he was a stand-up bloke and I didn't really get to know Kym Johnson, though I hear she's also a nice person.

I can't say the others left much of a positive impression on me and I expect they likely feel the same way. They were what I'd call fillers – they weren't going to set the world on fire or ever reach anywhere near the top of their profession. To the wider audience, they were realistically forgotten without having ever achieved anything for which they should be remembered.

There are many bit players in life who have the walk-ons and the non-speaking roles and it won't go beyond that. Sometimes it's bad luck, the interference of others, but most of the time it's just the result of a lack of talent. It's a terrible thing to want to be something, but not be good at it. I loved music and wanted to be a singer, and I was for a while, but I wasn't good enough to pursue it as a full-on career. I was also very ordinary at soccer and cricket, but what a terrible thing it is to find you're not really good enough to be more than you are. Like bikini models who discover they only have a career in front of the cameras while in a bikini – I've met a few of them.

The exception to that in the fillers of the *Survivor* cast was Justin Melvey. He had quite a few acting credits to his name, but more than that, he had a black belt in karate and was a sensational world-class snow skier. He'd had success in his life that I respected.

I've found a level of enjoyment from all the TV series I've done, but *Survivor* was my favourite. I almost thrived in the difficult conditions. Whilst many were having a bad time and suffered through the privations, including being very hungry a lot of the time, I found a lot of it quite relaxing.

I was used to the Australian bush and camping and being in out-of-the-way places. My interest in World War II had taken me all over the Pacific and I'd wandered through many sticky-creature and disease-infested jungles looking for artefacts. *Survivor* was filmed in Vanuatu and as it was my fourteenth trip to Vanuatu, I was familiar with the lay of the land there and what might be found or not found in the waters surrounding the island.

I was used to being clawed at with people wanting pieces of me day after day. There were days when my phone would ring fifty or more times and the media or other pollies would be trying to get me to do this and say that. Being in the jungle with no phones, newspapers, TV, radio or anyone who wanted me to fix something for them was quite therapeutic – I didn't even have a watch. However, quite a few of the others really struggled. By the end of the first forty-eight hours, some of the model types were very uncomfortable and may have done anything in return for a meal. One in particular was constantly demonstrating her lack of strength and vomiting here, there and everywhere.

Even the absence of coffee has its effect and there were those who were soon in serious withdrawal who would have killed for a latte. I don't drink coffee, so that and the fact I consume little if any refined sugar was helpful.

Throughout the series, producers would sit us down for one-on-one chats about who did what or how we were feeling, so we were kind of narrating as well as explaining events. Reality TV was in its infancy then and hence nowhere near as produced and manipulated as it is today. You pretty much got what was really going on, but one of the themes they did like to manage and depict was the struggle we had with the conditions.

Keep in mind, the only food we get is what we find or win. The only shelter is what we've built from brush and vines. We have only one change of clothes and we don't even have so much as a toothbrush – we learned to make them by shredding the end of little pieces of bamboo. Until we won some matting for the shelter, we were all sleeping huddled together on the sand. At one stage it rained for three days and I was wet through the whole time. I tried to sleep with my feet in a basket to at least keep them dry.

I will always remember being interviewed, sitting there in the jungle a couple of weeks into filming and the producer saying to me,

'It's pretty tough, you're not getting much to eat, you're sleeping rough and living hand to mouth. How do you feel?'

It was at that point I was expected to answer, 'Yeah, it's rough, I'm hungry and exhausted and stressed – it's pretty bad.' But, as I've said elsewhere, I always put what I'm feeling and experiencing in perspective.

What I did say was, 'Yeah, look it's tough and I could do with a good meal, but my dad was a prisoner of war with the Japanese. He was beaten, tortured, starving and had the threat of being murdered hanging over his head every day. Whereas, I'm okay – I'm not starving, no-one wants to kill me, and I know this program will end and I'll get to go home.'

It was a great line, because it was true, but, understandably, it never made the cut, as models throwing up was better vision for what the producers wanted to portray.

I loved *Survivor.* If at the end they'd asked me to start over, I would have done so happily. I won three individual immunity challenges, more than any other competitor, and I got down to the original final three, but my big mistake was I underestimated the stupidity of some people.

When there was a bikini model, a retired actress and me, I sat the girls down and explained to them that there were going to be new people come into the game. They asked, 'How do you know there will be new people?'

I told them how many days we had left and explained that there were too many days and not enough of us to cover those days based on the sequence of reward, challenge and elimination. I explained there could be changes in the sequence, but there were just too many days and they weren't going to simply film us lying around on the beach. They screamed, 'But that is not fair!'

To which I answered, 'Which part of all this did you think was going to be fair?'

I told them I didn't know whether there would be new people, or eliminated people reintroduced, but there would be at least one, maybe two people coming into the game. Apparently still stunned by my revelation, quite incredulously, they asked me, 'How do you know how many days are left?'

I told them what day it was and pointed out what day the program was due to finish and hence how I knew the number of days left. The bikini model and the retired actress seemed to have lost all track of time and had no idea of how long we'd been in the jungle – it was a complete blur to them. The notion of counting back over the sequence of challenges to establish a timeframe was also too much for them, as they pictured a breezy easy finish where they would simply dispose of me and one of them would win.

I explained there wasn't much chance there would be more than two people joining us and that we were three and three always outvotes two. All we had to do was stick together and even if one of the new people won immunity, we'd still have the numbers to vote out the other one. The next challenge there would be three of us, only one of them left and so the odds were on our side to win immunity, in which case we would vote off the last intruder and we would be back to the original final three. I explained that I understood they were a team and at that point they were free to gang up on me, so if I didn't win immunity in the following challenge, they would dispose of me, leaving the two of them to battle it out.

I was about to experience another example of how knowing what was likely to unfold didn't help me at all; in fact, it had the entirely opposite effect – it doomed me. This wasn't the first time I'd seen what was coming without it helping me and it wasn't the last time either, but this time was perhaps the most memorable.

The following day, we were summoned to watch a process that determined who would re-enter the jungle. As it turned out, it was two people, Guy Leech and Justin Melvey – two fit, strong guys who had just had a week in a resort relaxing and feeding up and were now in a much recovered state.

When what I'd explained would happen did happen exactly as I'd said, the two girls didn't sensibly embrace what I'd suggested we should do on the basis of three votes always beats two, no, they decided I was too smart and they had to get rid of me immediately. The effect of this would be to create a two-against-two situation, rather than the three of us in an alliance against the two intruders.

Guy and Justin explained to me that by working out what was going to happen well ahead of time, I'd frightened the girls and so they'd decided to join with Guy and Justin to dispose of me. The bikini model and the retired actress thought the smart play would be to breach their agreement with me because I was too dangerous, and get rid of me while they were sure of the numbers. According to Guy and Justin, the girls told them that would leave two against two for a fair fight to the end.

Guy thought they were mad, and we all knew these two girls lasting as long as they had wasn't as a consequence of any talent, so Guy and Justin offered me a deal to join them and get rid of the girls.

Silly me thought Guy and Justin were trying to play me and, as tempted as I was, I'd given my word to the girls that we'd stick together. I should have believed Guy, but I couldn't because at that time I couldn't see that anyone could be so imbecilic as to do what Guy said the girls were planning.

But Guy was telling the truth and the girls very foolishly voted to eliminate me and in doing so made themselves enormously vulnerable at the absolute pointy end of the game. As predicted, the two fit, strong, well-rested men, easily overcame the two weak, physically and mentally depleted girls, one by one, and ultimately, Guy Leech won with Justin running second. Despite being reintroduced into the game after being eliminated, Guy was a very worthy winner and it was my vote that got him over the line when it came down to him and Justin.

Only recently I saw a *Survivor* fan site where they rated me as the fourth best player out of the seventy-six players in the various Australian-related series of Survivor. I was quite chuffed about that, especially so as I was rated higher than the winners of my own series. It's nice to have one's work appreciated.

First Contact

As far as reality was concerned, it might have been a long time between drinks, but out of the blue I got a call from a lady wanting to gauge my interest in going bush to film a kind of 'celebrity' version of *First*

Contact. This was a program that took a group of non-Aboriginal Australians on a trip around the country, meeting and closely interacting with Aborigines. The idea was that participants were supposed to have not had any previous contact with Aborigines and hence the name *First Contact*. In theory, we would be confronted with what it was to be Aboriginal. To begin with, our views, or preconceived notions of Aborigines were gauged and recorded, then we would take off for a month and at the end, see if our views had changed.

The producers knew I'd had a lot to do with Aboriginal people, but it was certainly correct that I hadn't spent time with them in their own circumstances, in their homes and so on. There would be new experiences for me, just not to the same extent as the other 'celebrities'.

It was all a bit of a set up in many ways, you could see it a mile off – 'celebrities' meet Aborigines and see firsthand how difficult their lives are and of course said 'celebrities' become all emotional and essentially become advocates for the 'Aboriginal industry'. The producers clearly had an expectation that regardless of how one may have started the trip, by the end you'd be calling for more money and greater assistance for all things Aboriginal.

The production company was owned by Aborigines, so some might understandably take the view the entire premise was merely a front to indoctrinate the ignorant into being active participants in a propaganda exercise. Believe me, I know an exercise in propaganda when I see one.

The thing about 'celebrities' is that they often live in very catered-for worlds, largely devoid of any real perspective. Some just feel sorry for almost everyone, and those who don't care all that much want to appear to care, at least for the cameras. Don't choose to misunderstand me, I'm very compassionate. I'm also sentimental to an almost personally detrimental degree, but I try hard to not have my emotions run away with me. I look not just at a person's circumstances, but everything that surrounds them and how they're in the trouble they're in. Who is responsible? Are they taking any responsibility for their situation. So much to look at, so I will generally be initially sorry for what has befallen them, but my level of sympathy will be dependent on what

I discover about why things are as they are and what is being done to fix things.

Keeping in mind, these days, most realistic enquiries or questioning of any kind regarding Aborigines is generally met with someone screaming racist. It's something of a career killer most of the time, so 'celebs' tend to maintain a left-wing bleeding-heart facade, be it genuine or not.

It was quite a difficult decision to do *First Contact*. It wasn't a great period in my family life, the money was ordinary and I would be away from home for a month. That maybe doesn't sound that much trouble, but with me as the primary carer for my sons' needs and three horses to feed and take care of, as well as my dogs and parrot, I don't really like to go away.

To top it off, Lisa was unwell, but I'd gotten so far in, I didn't feel I could let the producers down. I shouldn't have felt that. The reality is I didn't owe them anything, but I'd committed to go and my own sense of doing what I say I'll do kept compelling me. I paid my boys' nanny to work seven days and nights to take up my duties and that kind of helped, but even today, I'm in two minds as to whether the decision to go was the right one.

The main thing playing on my mind was my concern that without me the whole series would be like an outback magical mystery tour for a bunch of celebs who didn't have a clue about Aborigines, crying their way through the whole thing and helping to build more misplaced guilt in the audience. Realistically, it was going to be an almost impossible task to find someone who wasn't going to drink the Kool Aid and go along with the producers' desire for the series to be a hug-fest of feeling sorry for Aboriginal people.

I do feel sorry for the circumstances a lot of Aboriginal people are in, but the problem with how Aboriginal issues are conveyed is that there's always an agenda to blame white people for everything, to apparently justify further demands for compensation. It was clear that if I didn't go, there wouldn't be anyone staying calm enough to point to the bleeding obvious that is always obscured by overactive and unjustified compassion, and the fear of being called racist.

As I'd noted, none of us were supposed to be at all familiar with Aboriginal people, yet we were supposed to hold ignorant views that would be broken down and changed through the experiences captured on film in the series. The whole objective of the production was to take a bunch of people and interview them about what they think of Aboriginal people, though they'd essentially not had anything to do with Aborigines and perhaps not even met one.

While no-one would admit to it, the producers' expectation and indeed, hope, was that everyone would have such an eye-opening experience that their view of Aboriginal people would completely change. That is change from a position of fear, misunderstanding and possibly racism based on ignorance, to an informed view where they had come to respect Aborigines and be dazzled by their culture and society; amazed by their 'one-ness' with the land.

That would have worked out perfectly too because that is pretty much how it panned out for the other five 'adventurers' in the group. For a couple of them it was real; however, I suggest the others were somewhat sorry for Aborigines, but a little part of their reaction to the overall 'journey' was a politically correct act conjured up so as not to jeopardise their careers.

The spanner in the works was me. Why they wanted me on the program, and they fought hard to get me, is a bit of a mystery, though I suspect not having at least one doubting Thomas along for the ride may have seemed like just a bit too much of a set-up.

I think there's also a chance the producers thought they might turn me to the light – that's the light as they see it. Perhaps they were so believing of their own spin they couldn't imagine I wouldn't come around to their way of thinking?

However, I wasn't ignorant of Aboriginal affairs. I'd spent a lot of time looking at Aboriginal issues and dealt with many Aboriginal people both officially and personally – for a while, I dated an Aboriginal girl while working in Queensland. I hadn't been to Arnhem Land and to far-flung Aboriginal settlements and I hadn't met Aboriginal people in the wilds of the outback, but I'd advised on Aboriginal studies while working for Tony Abbott and spent a good deal of time with Aboriginal government staff. I'd also made quite a study of the anthropological history of Australia and the early interactions, good and bad, between them and the colonists. Indeed, I'd made numerous speeches in parliament related to Aboriginal issues. I didn't start the program ignorant of all things Aboriginal, like the others, but rather, I was very familiar with Aborigines and the issues related to them.

I spent a month solid on the road meeting Aboriginal artists, workers, business people, trainees, children, those claiming stolen generation status, the unwell, the privileged and the welfare recipients. I didn't see or hear anything that changed my views. If anything, everything I saw and heard had the effect of strongly reinforcing the views I'd formed over years of experience I'd already had in Aboriginal affairs.

Perhaps you might baulk at the idea of privileged Aborigines, but only because you don't know they exist. Yet, they're there, the Aborigines who make a lot of money through the special status they enjoy amongst other Aborigines. I met a couple of them during the filming of *First Contact*. One in particular really stands out. She sat down with us to tell us, indeed, educate us, on the hardship endured by her community. There she sat before us, the wonder of the Australian countryside as a marvellous backdrop – extraordinary images, perfect for filming. It all appeared so natural, so Australian.

She reminded me of a pallbearer from White Lady Funerals, not the dealing in death part that is their business, but the way she was so impeccably dressed – the perfectly tailored white outfit and even the broad brimmed maroon hat, and she was utterly dripping in over-the-top gold jewellery and a chunky gold designer watch. It's great to see success, but it seemed somewhat incongruous given she was conveying the hardship of her tiny community yet not exhibiting any of that hardship herself.

When I questioned her, it became apparent she owned numerous businesses in the little township, including the only liquor outlet, and needless to say, none of those scenes made it into the series and onto the TV screens of Australia.

When we visited an Aboriginal housing estate, we saw the appalling level of filth in which this group of people choose to live – yeah, I said, 'choose to live', because all the filth had been created by them, no-one else. The houses and yards were just dumping grounds for every day rubbish, bottles, cans, plastic wrappers and discarded packaging of every kind, just dropped – in some places it was nearly a foot deep. Also, there were old mattresses, tyres and I suppose whatever else wasn't wanted in the house, just tossed outside to build up in the yard. The other houses in the area were the same. Even the kids' playground was littered in a similar fashion, including large amounts of broken glass – one child cut their foot while we were there.

This was all rubbish created by the occupants of the homes, yet it was lost on my fellow cast members that it was the Aborigines who had made the mess. They were sympathising with the perpetrators as if they were victims and calling for someone to clean up the mess for them. Had they not been Aborigines, everyone would have just agreed the people who lived in these taxpayer-supplied homes were pigs, but no, when it's Aboriginal people many advocate they're not responsible for anything. Not even responsible for picking up their own rubbish. I didn't take the, 'Sorry I'm white and have caused you to make a mess line' and I asked them why they didn't clean up.

I took it a step further and suggested that when you adopt the attitude of not dropping rubbish, then there isn't any to clean up. Well, wasn't I the worst bloke they'd ever met, and rude as well!

Another house we visited had a bathroom that looked like a bomb site. One of the cast labelled it the dirtiest bathroom in Australia and was appalled by the terrible conditions, once again unwilling to note the people who got it so dirty were the occupants of the house.

We also visited a home belonging to a part Aboriginal family who had a business and were doing okay and their home was neat, tidy and well maintained, but that was the exception. Was it the exception because they had jobs and self-worth and weren't living off taxpayers and complaining, but rather, making something for themselves? A matter for you to consider.

We stayed on a beach in the far north with a local clan who even had a sort of pet crocodile that I hand fed. The producers were aghast that I took that risk, but, hey, that's how I am – a calculated risk after observing behaviour. Was there danger? It's a cold-blooded man-eating reptile. The only thing you can predict about them is they're largely unpredictable and hence dangerous, but as I teach my sons, don't be afraid of anything, but be careful of everything.

I even made a video of it and narrated it as I did it to teach my boys about calculated risk. Do I want them hand feeding a 4-metre saltwater crocodile within lunging distance? *No*, but it wasn't really about the crocodile as such.

We were on the beach for three nights. In the program, it was sort of billed as experiencing traditional Aboriginal lifestyle, but apart from donning some ochre and dancing around a fire, there wasn't anything related to traditional Aboriginal lifestyle. We had hot showers, refrigeration and catering three meals a day, where we lined up with the 'traditional Aborigines' for the food cooked on gas appliances by the white catering staff.

None of that appeared in the series, though they did show the Aborigines fishing 'traditionally', with a polystyrene floated nylon drag net. Very traditional; it's a little-known fact polystyrene and nylon were invented during the Stone Age.

They took everything they caught. When I suggested a level of sustainability might be releasing the very much undersized fish, I was treated as if I'd been in the sun too long. Seriously, the conversation ended with the head Aborigine saying to me, 'Put 'em back? We just caught 'em!'

The series showed the fishing and the cooking of this one catch and portrayed it as if it was how we hunted and ate for the whole time we were there. Strangely, there was no vision of us all lining up each morning for our bacon and eggs hot off the grill.

At another point in our traditional stay, the cast marvelled at bush medicine. This is where ignorant white people who've taken on the notion there's something natural missing from their lives are astounded by the boiling of a few leaves picked from 'special trees' by wise, all-knowing Aborigines. When the cooked leaves and related juice is rubbed on your skin it soothes all manner of things.

There is the chance you're falling for this too, so I'll add a touch of reality to this crazy notion of special healing powers. I've been in the bush and the jungle and met different native peoples around the world, and they all pretty much have versions of this – some better than others. In some case, there are natural alternatives to aspirin and a range of natural ingredients for reducing pain and so on, but that's beyond the boiled leaves and smoke we got given.

You're likely familiar with the gel of medicinal aloe vera plants. Great stuff. Better than a few boiled leaves from the Arnhem Land Aborigines. Soothes sunburn and bug bites and the like, and you can juice it – great for rehydrating. So, there's nothing new or unique about Aboriginal bush medicine. There are similar things all over the world and they have a place as a topical treatment, but if you've got a burst appendicitis, rub as much as you like on your belly, but you're still gonna die! Such sense, however, has little impact on easily impressed white people who are convinced they've somehow long lost their connection to Mother Earth. They like the idea there's something better in the bush than what might be found in modern medicine.

This crazy feeling of wanting to reconnect with the earth and that this might be achieved with the help of 'native peoples' is probably taking up some of the ground in people's minds that used to be occupied by religion. A bit of smoke and hot leaves and a massage and the next thing the cast of *First Contact* are hallucinating and feeling all native deep down in their souls – except for me of course.

At another moment, one of our Aboriginal companions turned to a couple of us, pointed to the ground and said, 'You must respect this land, it's 40,000 years old.'

As nicely as I could, I said, 'Try billions. It's actually billions of years old, not 40,000 years.'

He looked at me curiously, not at all getting what I meant; and why would he, given he was equating the age of the land with his understanding of what he'd been taught about how long Aboriginal people had been there. He explained he'd been told Aborigines had been there 40,000 years – did he extrapolate that to then also being the age of the land in that it didn't exist before his people occupied it?

It's hard to tell what he'd thought up himself, but what I do know is the Aborigines had no written language or form of recording anything. Indeed, anthropologically, it's largely accepted Aborigines have only had language for 4000 years. Once again, the non-Aborigines who fall for the hokum of shows such as *First Contact* don't seem to take into account that all the details of Aboriginal occupation of the land have been determined by specialist science, archaeologists, anthropologists and so on, not by any information from Aborigines. Typically, it had for a long time been generally suggested Aborigines first arrived in Australia 40,000 years ago and hence the figure used by our Arnhem Land companion. So, we were being briefed by a well-meaning fellow who was taken by the rest of the cast to be of great knowledge, but in fact, didn't really have a clue.

A similar thing occurred in relation to didgeridoos. One of our Arnhem Land companions was impressing on us the need to respect the didgeridoo, as it was the oldest musical instrument in the world. I felt like asking where they got this bullshit from, but just like I dealt with the age of the land, I said, 'People were banging sticks together and beating makeshift drums a long time before anyone made a didgeridoo.'

Again, such thoughts were lost on them. Perhaps because for so long they've been told they are the oldest people in the world that they presume anything they have is the oldest of its kind.

As I write this, I wonder if any Aborigines are aware the oldest boomerangs in the world have been found in Poland. Perhaps I should have raised that at the time, but the invention of boomerangs never came up. I imagine most people, Aboriginal and otherwise, think boomerangs are exclusively an Australian thing, or at least an Aboriginal invention, but in fact they've been found in many places around the world.

At the end of our three days and nights living 'traditionally' with Aborigines, we packed up to leave to film elsewhere. The Aborigines packed too – they loaded their 4WDs, the traditional transport of Aborigines, and headed back to town, where their real homes were.

On *First Contact,* I met Aboriginal people who were genuinely trying to make a difference for themselves and for other Aboriginal people as well. I also met Aborigines who take every advantage of being Aboriginal. They are the ones who are smart enough to do well for themselves and unscrupulous enough to take from those around them, just as non-Aborigines do.

Then there were those who will never amount to anything more than parasites on the public purse. They will drain government funding their whole lives and by example, if not intentionally, teach their children to do the same. The parasite group of Aborigines, are just like the many non-Aborigines who bludge in a similar way. That's the thing, when it comes down to human responses to situations, Aborigines have a lot in common with non-Aborigines, there are the good, the bad and the ugly.

I'd noted there wasn't anything I saw or heard on *First Contact* that changed my views – if anything the views I'd formed over years of experience in Aboriginal issues, were sustained and reinforced.

However, there was a particular cast member who criticised me for not changing my views after all I'd seen. Firstly, it may have been lost on him that I didn't see anything I considered new, whereas he hadn't seen any of these things before – the whole experience was new for him. He'd started with the typical trendy, politically correct view that Aborigines were the victims of white aggression, colonisation and racist policies and without any responsibility for their own circumstances. And of course there is an argument in that when none of it is balanced with context and historical fact. It's a view one reaches when they only have a bit of the story or they've seen the result without knowing how it came about. His whole position was brought about without any practical experience or knowledge, but now he'd seen a few things and his view had also remained unchanged. He still had the same views he had before he started on the series.

As he criticised me for not having changed my position I pointed out to him that he hadn't changed his either, but this was lost on him – I was wrong not to have changed yet he was right not to have changed, the extraordinary hypocrisy that those who perpetrate it can never see.

Doing *First Contact* wasn't an enjoyable experience, but it was valuable in being able to critically evaluate the views I'd formed and reassess the conclusions I'd reached about Aboriginal affairs. In the end, I was the villain. In fact, I was the villain at the beginning, in the middle and at the end. I have no doubt the producers wanted me so the series would have at least one dissenting voice, one non-believer to add some level of credibility to the falsehood that this was a series truly aimed at genuine outcomes of informed thought.

At the same time, however, I'm of the view they thought they'd change my views; that I would be so moved that I too would become a true believer. I guess they just didn't have any idea how strongly I rationally hold on and never let a sad outcome hide the facts of how things happen or who is responsible.

It would have been easy to be swayed, to lose all my principles, to let go of my understanding of the application of context and perspective and just cry and be sorry and loved for my misplaced empathy and compassion, but I don't go along to get along. That said, I sometimes wish I could do that. I sometimes wish I could cast all sense and fairness of evaluation to one side and join the sobbing mob support for serial victimhood, but no matter how deep I mine, I just can't unearth that willingness to deceive.

I've been told I'm honest to the point of my own detriment, and finally, after all these years, I know that isn't a good thing for me personally, so I'm going to try hard to make sure my sons never put themselves out there as I have done my whole life. In this, it's not in their interests for them to be like me.

The Real Housewives of Sydney

No, I've really always seen myself as a widow rather than a divorcee.

– Lisa Oldfield,
when asked if she could see herself divorcing me

In 2015, my wife Lisa was cast in *The Real Housewives of Sydney*. If you've ever seen any of the many Real Housewives franchises, Sydney, Melbourne, Beverley Hills, New York ... then you'll know the women in these shows are anything but real housewives.

Apologies in advance, but the cold hard truth is that no-one is interested in the drudgery of real housewives. I know this because while some have referred to me as the seventh housewife, I'm very much a house husband, so I know all about the day-to-day chores. Getting the kids up for school, feeding them, popping them in the bath, brushing their teeth, packing their school bags and driving them to school. The washing and being sure their uniforms are ready to go and their shoes are polished. The shopping and after-school activities, dinner, bathing and teeth brushing again and finally lights out. And repeat and repeat – you get the picture. No-one wants to watch others on the treadmill they're on themselves, the same daily grind. They want to watch what they consider to be the exciting lives others live and that they'd like to live as well.

The big houses, the lavish lifestyles, fancy cars and restaurants, private schools, plush surroundings, international high-quality travel, the staff, the clothes, the jewellery, the Jimmy Choos! It's escape, or as the producers call it 'aspirational television'.

Then there's the gay following. All these shows have huge gay audiences. I imagine it's because the programs showcase powerful women. Gays love powerful women, or at least that's what I'm told, but it's not my place to speak on behalf of gay guys.

I had quite a bit of screen time. I was certainly the most featured husband, which made sense, as Lisa created more than her share of the drama and of course I was a big part of that. Our children, our house, our animals all got a run. I don't think we had any family secrets left by the end of the series and I'm sure we left plenty of people with entirely the wrong impression of the dynamic of our relationships and how our lives operate.

I'm not convinced about exactly what the effect of it all was on our family, but it probably wasn't great. It was a very difficult time for Lisa, which made all our lives torturous, though I mostly shield the boys from that, nowadays if not before.

There'd never been a housewife like Lisa Oldfield before – she said that would be the case before the show went to air, and she was true to her word. The angst and bitterness between Lisa and me is something rarely if ever recorded for TV audience consumption, but there it was for all to see. The show directed a spotlight on the horror of our marriage and likely allowed many other couples the opportunity to see they're not on their own when it comes to trouble and ugliness within their own relationship. Still, the vision and words only scratched the surface, and like so many of these things, much of the truth ended up on the cutting room floor, and much of what I could have disclosed, I never did.

Hell's Kitchen

> Coconut – because he's really hard and very scratchy on the outside, but he's quite secretly sweet on the inside, deep on the inside. I had a couple of moments with David that he didn't show Australia.
>
> – Debra Lawrance,
> Logie-award-winning actress and winner of *Hell's Kitchen,*
> describing me on the *Morning Show* on Channel Seven,
> 28 August 2017

In early 2017, I got the call from Channel Seven to be in the first series of their new program, *Hell's Kitchen*. By chance, I'd seen a few moments of the British version because my friend, actress Kelly LeBrock, had been cast.

Frankly, I really wasn't in the right headspace to be doing a series – I wasn't sleeping, I felt sluggish and I was consuming Glucodin (glucose based product) most days to give myself an energy hit. But the money was good and I thought it would be a chance to do something a bit out of the ordinary for me, in that there wouldn't be any political overtones.

There was also the fact that I like to cook but my food has always been prepared on the basis of 'food is fuel' because for me, food is about nutrition, anti-cancer benefits, antioxidants and so on, rather than taste.

The star of the series was the chef in charge, he who would guide us through *Hell's Kitchen,* and that was Marco Pierre White, probably the greatest chef of his generation. The chance to learn from Marco Pierre White would probably never come along again, so it wasn't hard to talk me into signing on.

At the age of thirty-three, Marco received three Michelin stars. He was the youngest chef ever to be recognised in this way. He has often been called the original celebrity chef and was noted not only for his arguably unparalleled excellence in the kitchen, but also his temper. World famous chef, Gordon Ramsay, was his apprentice. Marco is said to have been the only person to ever make Ramsay cry. Of that, Marco said to me, 'To be fair to Gordon, he was peeling onions at the time.'

Here was a chance to swing myself towards taste. Especially given I do almost all the cooking for my sons, the chance to get better and faster at it was too good an opportunity to miss.

'David, your eggs are overcooked,' Marco Pierre White told me on my first day in *Hell's Kitchen*. I responded, 'My children like them.' And Marco said, 'Children like their eggs overcooked.'

I cook simple meals for my sons. To try and cater in any way other than simply for them will just lead to them not eating what is prepared and then having them fall back on rice crackers or similar snacks. I learned early on to get nutrients into them through means including camouflaging vegetables in mince or beans, as I'm sure most parents do, but I also back up with supplements.

I eat concentrated tomato paste by the spoonful straight out of the jar, raw vegetables, brazil nuts, dark chocolate and or raw cacao, eggs, lots of the right oils, black cumin seeds, turmeric, and that's every day – there are specific things I eat every day regardless of where I am or what I'm doing. That's how I was before *Hell's Kitchen* and I still am, but the difference now is that I take extra time to make my daily nutritional intake tasty, and when it comes to seriously cooking for others, taste takes priority.

Marco gave me an appreciation for seasoning, for the proper preparation of garlic and for throwing a dinner party where the attendees take home the view they've had high-quality, restaurant-level cuisine from my kitchen.

One thing I now commonly make is Café de Paris butter, including actually churning the butter from cream. I put that in a range of things. It's so versatile – even my sons get it in their scrambled eggs. My own personality being one that largely strives for perfection, combined with the enthusiasm that Marco inspired in me, has made a phenomenal difference to everything I prepare.

I liked Marco very much. He was billed as a real tough nut, but I found him an intelligent fellow who was very much a gentleman. I got to know him reasonably well and frankly, found we had a great deal in common. We were about the same age, we're somewhat 'old school', we were both focused on being dads, we were both students of human behaviour and we both had a huge interest in history, especially things military.

Admittedly, I was surprised when one night I heard him tell a customer, 'Go away madam, you are embarrassing yourself,' but if he was ever a real hard arse, he has clearly mellowed with age.

When I say customer, I mean in the sense of a diner, as *Hell's Kitchen* was a show where we 'celebrities' were expected to be cooks and kitchen hands in a restaurant built in a sound stage at Channel Seven's studios. We put on three-course lunches and dinners for up to 120 guests and depending on our performance, we might finish up chosen by Marco to go into a last chance cook-off where the loser would be eliminated from the program.

The cast was reasonable in terms of so-called celebrity status, especially given these days celebrity appears to mean having a claim to being known beyond your own family, circle of friends and acquaintances. There were ten of us altogether, and of the ten, I was aware of six, counting me. How many would I have passed in the street and recognised? Probably none, but they weren't people from things that interested me as such, so I'm not a good guide to how well known they were.

Did I get along with the others? To greater and lesser degrees. That's often misinterpreted though, as in when I said, 'None of the cast are really my sort of people, so I wouldn't expect to catch up with them after the series.' That was taken by some to be nasty, whereas, it was just a fact that I suggest applied equally to me from the other cast members' point of view.

There would also be some among the cast who departed the program with the view I didn't like them, but they probably concluded that from what they thought was my view of them, rather than my real feelings toward them. The truth is, there were some I thought of as fillers, some I liked, some I respected, and at least one I admired, but I suspect they'd have terrible trouble working out who was in which category, because for the most part, they'd likely think I thought very little of any of them. I didn't actually dislike any of my fellow cast. I'd happily have a drink and a chat with any of them, though a few of them likely don't feel the same.

We started *Hell's Kitchen* in two teams who competed for the approval of the diners. The team scoring the least points would have a member selected by Marco and that person would find themselves in the cook-off up against two other celebs, chosen through the same means.

When I did *Survivor* back in 2006, reality TV was still relatively young and not heavily manipulated by producers, but by the time I got to *Hell's Kitchen* in 2017, there'd been so many varieties of reality TV that in many respects the genre had evolved toward a type of drama created by scripting and behind the scenes manipulation. I got through one cook-off and should have made it through the second as well, but that hadn't been the plan for me and so I found myself on the wrong end of a departure from the rules that had been previously clearly established. There was also a question mark over whether I should have even been in the cook-off from which I was eliminated, but that's just the way it went down.

Could I have won *Hell's Kitchen*? Emphatically, no – apart from not being in the right frame of mind at the time, I just wasn't good enough in the kitchen. Should I have been eliminated when I was? Also, no, but if I hadn't been, I would have been likely eliminated in the next couple of eliminations, so it wasn't a big deal.

When it was happening and it was obvious it was going to be me, I was professional, gracious and even cheerful in accepting the umpire's decision, because, there wasn't any practical purpose in being any other way. When you're going and there's no way to change that, no matter how improper the circumstances may be, go happily, go in style and wish the others the best – to do otherwise is unproductive.

I didn't love doing *Hell's Kitchen*, but I liked it enough to feel okay about it and I did meet some very good people who were in the crew and working with Marco. Of course, meeting and being inspired by Marco, well, that made it more than worthwhile.

'David.'

'Yes Marco.'

'Your meatballs, beautifully shaped, good sauce.'

'Thank you Marco.'

'I could taste the Manchego [Spanish cheese from sheep milk] and I could taste the parsley.'

'Thank you Marco.'

'The meatball itself, was dry and dense.'

'David.'

'Yes Marco.'

'You have done so well.'

'Thank you Marco.'

'But what brought you down in the end, was putting the flour in the meatball mix.'

'Yes Marco.'

'It was a pleasure working with you, cooking with you and spending time with you.'

'The pleasure was entirely mine Marco. Thank you very much for having me.'

Such was my final conversation with Marco on *Hell's Kitchen*.

Being as I am, the first thing I cooked when I exited the program was indeed, Meatballs Manchego. With a little experimentation, I perfected the recipe and now my meatballs are the most moist you will find anywhere – they melt in one's mouth.

I'm a Celebrity ... Get Me Out of Here!

They say be careful what you wish for, and never say never, and that was certainly the case for me one Tuesday night.

From time to time there are international news outlets that interview me on apparently controversial matters where some appearance of balance is required, so I get picked as the conservative view.

I was doing one of those at 9.30 pm this night and the media agency, which was headquartered in London, had hired a studio at Channel Ten in Sydney for the live cross. On the way in, the reality show *I'm a Celebrity … Get Me Out of Here!* was playing on the screen near the security station and in casual conversation, I said to the guy on security, 'Of all the reality programs I might do, that is the one I would never do. I could never eat the maggots, flies and other stuff they dish up on that show.'

The very next day, Wednesday, about 1 pm, my mobile rings and when I answer, I hear a voice say, 'David, it's Ben.'

I reasonably presume Ben thought I had his number programmed into my phone and would immediately know which Ben, but I didn't, so when I hesitated for a second, he said, 'Ben Ulm.'

Ben, the head of content for ITV, was calling from South Africa, and that was all he had to say for me to guess why he was calling. Ben had his phone on speaker and was in the company of Stephen Tate, head of entertainment and factual programs for Channel Ten, the TV channel that airs *I'm a Celebrity … Get Me Out of Here!*

Less than twenty-four hours earlier I was telling a security officer at Channel Ten that I would never do *I'm a Celebrity … Get Me Out of Here!* and now the people making the program are on the phone asking me to drop everything and fly to the other side of the world!

They'd decided that Lisa and I would be the first ever married couple to enter the jungle. And so the problems raised their heads. Our little sons had never been separated from both parents at once except when Albert was only twelve months old and he stayed at home with his nanny while the rest of us went to New Zealand for a few days of skiing. This was a whole new ball game as both boys were now in school and needed to be catered for in so many other ways as well.

Even being happy we could sort our boys, then there was the matter of us having ten pets, four of which are horses – one cannot just leave a pile of hay in the middle of the paddock and skedaddle for a few weeks!

This was Wednesday afternoon, and at that stage they wanted us on an 11 am flight on Friday. Included in what was less than forty-eight hours, we were to have medical assessments, physical and psychological. I keep passing the psychological tests? Yes I know, it's a mystery to me as well! Plus there were wardrobe fittings, publicity shoots and to top it off, my doctor decides he's unhappy with my heart and insists I have an ECG – don't get your hopes up, my heart has an irregular beat, but it's perfectly fine. My doctor knows that, but he was concerned about me being in the jungle and so removed from a major first world hospital, so fair enough. All checked out and surprise, surprise, once again, it was confirmed I have a heart– indeed, an unusually strong heart.

There was also the matter of visas to enter South Africa, and to achieve that, the producers had to pick up our passports and have a staffer fly all around, including to Canberra to get that sorted. Oh, did I mention Lisa's passport had expired???

We had a mother-daughter act, cousins from Perth, come to stay to look after our little boys and feed the smaller pets and I sent our horses off to agistment at a nearby stable.

Channel Ten were very good with all they had to do, and given their need and our inconvenience, also came to the party with the right money, so it was all good and we managed a 3 am limo pick-up on the Saturday for a 6 am departure. We were flat out without a break, but we got it done – I didn't go to bed on the Friday night, but by the time our driver arrived, I was comfortable every detail had been covered and we could sink into the leather seats of the limo, with a sigh of relief, knowing everything was under control.

We had a good flight (I still enjoy flying) and after a very long haul including a stop-off in Dubai, we landed in Johannesburg.

Why go via Dubai you might quite rightly ask? *I'm a Celebrity … Get Me Out of Here!* is partly filmed live, so unlike all the other reality TV I'd done, this show was already being broadcast before we joined in, so we had to sneak onto the set. Stopping in Dubai, rather than flying directly to South Africa, was a way to throw off the paparazzi as to who was on their way to the jungle.

Channel Ten had been teasing the audience with promos that Australia's most dysfunctional couple were about to intrude on the other unsuspecting celebrities. Are we Australia's most dysfunctional couple? It's fair to say it's somewhat ugly at times. Lisa likes to say, 'We put the fun in dysfunctional.'

We entered the jungle camp with much fanfare yet mystery as we were each concealed in a large box and wheeled into the midst of the curious 'celebrities'. The casts of these shows don't like intruders at the best of times – there is a sort of togetherness that builds up between those who started the show and generally the audience are mostly rusted on to people who started on day one.

It was a bit of a double whammy for the cast of, *I'm a Celebrity ... Get Me Out of Here!* With the exception of the two cast members from England, they all knew who we were and, quite understandably, they had preconceived ideas of what we would be like. Not only were we late in the series intruders, but we were considered very controversial and for some of the cast, it was a bit too much for them to handle.

Like all these shows, most of the people on them are very left wing or at least toeing the politically correct line, so there is always going to be conflict with me if they make the mistake of asking questions for which they don't really want my answers. However, between encouragement from producers and their own foolish curiosity, they can't help themselves and so the poo hits the fan because, as you may have gathered, I don't hold back in sharing my views.

This, however, was why we were there. Everyone in the camp had settled into napping, conversation had dried up and the camp had the feel of having just had the plague pass through. The stench of death was everywhere – not good television. The program was suffering in the ratings and we were specifically chosen to spice things up, stir things up, heat things up, and we did.

We got them talking again; we got them energised and we got them involved. Most of them would probably not see it or admit it, but the producers were very happy with our work. I got into arguments with a couple of the cast, Lisa and I fought regularly on camera and, as expected, we polarised the audience and created huge amounts of rage and media back in Australia. Yep, the producers got from us exactly what they were after and made a point of letting us know.

I was hopeful the jungle would be therapeutic for Lisa, and it turned out to be a bit that way, even though at the end she announced publicly she was divorcing me. Was she really thinking that? Hard to tell, but it surely did get the show a lot of extra publicity.

It was all a bit of a cruise for me as far as jungle life was concerned and I didn't suffer the privations the others did. I enjoyed my short stay – it reminded me a little of *Survivor*, but nowhere near as difficult. The food was regular and okay, there was very little expected of us and we had all the comforts of a nice camping trip in our little village; goodness, we had hard frame hammocks! I spent *Survivor* on the hard ground and a lot of the time it was wet. To be frank, it was easy, but just as I'd noted when I said I'd never do this show, the jungle cuisine in the challenges was my only problem.

I don't care about spiders and insects and snakes. I'm careful of things, but I'm not frightened of creatures. Even the prospect of bumping into leopards or the ever-present violent baboons didn't faze me one little bit. After all, if I was confronted by a deadly animal, I would have calmly grabbed whoever was close to me and put them between me and the predator. I'm kidding of course – or am I?!

However, the prospect of eating cockroaches or scorpions, camels' testicles or fresh raw pigs intestines and similar awful ugly things is an entirely different matter. Personally, I'd choose a nice meal of roasted human flesh over any of that other garbage. Again, I'm kidding – or am I?

I knew what I was in for, so I just steeled myself for the fact I'd have to eat whatever they gave me and that was that. As it turned out, I was fortunate that the only thing I had to stomach was eating a bull's eye – yuk! A decidedly ugly experience. I thought, okay, can't be that bad, I'll just swallow it fast and get it done, but noooo, a bull's eye is too big to swallow. It was much bigger than my oesophagus – there was no way it could be swallowed whole.

Confronted with the size of the damn thing, my plan was out the window, so what the hell, I have to do it, and I grab it and try to bite it in half. That didn't work either. It's muscle and sinew and of course there's the lens and the retina – I don't recommend trying this at home boys and girls.

It was about a minute on TV, though it actually took me around fifteen minutes to chew the damn eyeball into small enough pieces to swallow, and the whole time I was gagging and dry retching. When later asked on camera by the hosts about the experience, I said, 'I've been shot, stabbed, glassed, had 20 per cent of my body burned, been blown up and had decompression sickness twice, and eating that bull's eye was worse than all of those things.'

Realistically, I'm not sure it was worse than all those things, and I'm not sure the hosts realised I was serious about those experiences, but I won't be eating another bull's eye any time soon! The difference was no doubt that the other occasions were unplanned and unexpected whereas with the bull's eye, I had the option of opting out, but didn't.

Like previous shows, the cast were a cross-section of sport and entertainment personalities – some very well known, some not so much. Again, there wasn't anyone I disliked as such, though there were a couple I didn't really have time for, and whilst I'd still say hi or sit down for a chat, I wouldn't miss them if I didn't bump into them again. I'm generally friendly-ish and courteous, but I tend not to pretend I particularly like someone if I don't.

When one watches the show, it becomes evident who were the backstabbers and those who would say anything to help themselves along. That's always part of the experience of these programs – the decency shown to your face is often undermined by what you later see of what they said to the camera when you weren't around.

Josh Gibson, a retired, but great AFL player is a fellow horse enthusiast, so perhaps we'll have a ride some time and Lisa made friends with Paul Burrell, the renowned butler of Princess Diana. Danny Green, three times world boxing champion, has already brought his lovely family to our home for lunch. I like and admire Danny. He is what Americans would call a 'real stand-up guy'. He has kind of an old-style warrior's code – he isn't the sort of person who gets led into saying things others want him to say, and he's a gentleman. Danny's also a hell of a fighter and I had him impress upon my seven-year-old son Henry, the importance of making a proper fist. Henry has just started doing the karate style I did as a kid, so it was a great lesson.

My stay in the jungle was relatively brief – just a week and I was out, eliminated by an audience charged with voting to keep their favourite. That's how it works, and I didn't mind, I preferred to go before Lisa, so it worked out well. Things weren't great at home, so it was very helpful that I wasn't in the jungle for long. I got home to get everything straight again before Lisa returned.

Did I feel bad about being eliminated so early? Not at all. The voting is based on saving your favourite and neither Lisa nor I had enough time to sway an audience who had been rusted on to others for several weeks before we interrupted the silence. I had the experience, I got to play round-up with a wild zebra, met some great people, got paid well enough and managed to get home before our children or animals suffered, so all good.

All the main people involved in the production were very clear they were thankful for what we'd done. Individually and together, they told us we'd achieved all they hoped we would. Of the twenty-two episodes counting from the week prior to when we entered the jungle until the announcement of the winner at the end of the series, the only notable increase in ratings related directly to us. The ratings bottomed out with our arrival and started recovering while we were in the jungle, dropping after we were eliminated.

The people who hate Lisa and me can't see how many others love to watch our antics, get the dark humour and find us entertaining. For the most part, it's lost on a lot of people that those who polarise, tend to garner the most interest. Once Lisa and I were gone, so was a large portion of the audience. None of the following seven elimination segments went close to ours. In fact, those final seven eliminations were mostly 100,000–150,000 viewers fewer than our eliminations, despite what should have been the expected excitement as the series was drawing to a close.

The End is Nigh

The world as we know it will come to an end at 2300 hours Eastern Standard Time on 17 April 2023. How do I know that? I don't, it's ridiculous, clearly. I don't know when the world will come to an end and neither does anyone else. There is however the matter of defining what is meant by 'as we know it'. Some might argue this has already happened to a degree.

My dear father used to say, 'Son, the whole world's gone mad.' It was his way of saying people were utterly off the rails with the things they said, did, believed and pursued. I think it's fair to say that before my parents died, the world as they knew it had come to an end and perhaps that's how it is for every generation, or at least for those who live long enough to see changes that to them make absolutely no sense.

I already feel that way about changes in the world, so I know how my dad felt and I've still got many years ahead of me – well as far as I know I have, but if you know different, give me a heads-up so I can make sure I'm not wherever I'm supposed to be when my end comes.

We don't even know when we'll go ourselves. I remember that great retort used by a lot of smokers, Lisa included. When confronted with the fact that 50 per cent of smokers will die of a smoking-related disease, Lisa says, 'So what, 100 per cent of people are going to die anyway be they smokers or not.'

Lisa is right, but the horrible, weak cancer-riddled death experienced as a consequence of smoking is not only ugly, debilitating and painful, but it tends to cut many years off what otherwise might have been a long, healthy life. Don't try to reason with smokers – most know someone who smoked all their life and lived to be 100, or they know someone who knows someone who smoked all their life and lived to be 100.

My answer to that is, 'Well, imagine how long they'd have lived if they hadn't smoked.'

It's true, something is going to kill us. In fact, most of us will die from the same thing, extreme hypoxia. This is where something cuts the flow of oxygen to the brain and it's how the vast majority of people will ultimately succumb. There are many ways for this to happen – heart attack, poisoning, stroke, violence such as that which causes a wound or trauma – the end result is the same, the restriction or shutting down of blood flow and hence an impediment to the flow of oxygen to the brain.

But this chapter isn't about death of individuals as such, it's about the death of, 'life as we know it'. And to that I will add, I don't have a plan for dying, I have a plan for living. It's a line I always use when those pesky telemarketers call me to enquire as to whether I have funeral insurance. I always say, 'No, I don't need funeral insurance, I'm not planning on dying.' Then I hang up the phone. Oh, I say goodbye nicely first.

It's reasonable to say humankind is in more danger of bringing about the end of the world as we know than at any other time in history. That's not to say there weren't other times in history when the end, so to speak, couldn't have been brought about. In fact, it's really all a matter of scale. In ancient times, and not so ancient times, whole villages were snuffed out without a trace being left by roving bands of killers – that's so much more than the world as we know it coming to an end. For those people, that was their world coming to an end. They and their existence disappeared without trace and in many cases there is no record of those people ever having lived.

The horror visited on the villagers of Lidice in 1942 is terrible beyond belief and for those who suffered yet survived, it truly was the end of the world as they knew it. The Nazis murdered every male over fifteen years of age (192) and sent all the women and children to concentration camps or other diabolical institutions, where many were systematically eliminated. Then a team was sent in to erase forever all evidence Lidice had ever stood. They used explosives and fire to level the buildings and covered the area with soil and planted crops. They even rerouted the stream that ran through the town and the roads leading to and from the town, so there would be nothing to suggest anything had ever stood there. Even the livestock and pets of Lidice were slaughtered and those buried in the cemetery were disinterred and robbed of valuables such as the gold in their teeth. Most of the women survived the war, but only 17 of the 105 children were still alive. Those left, returned, but to what? Most certainly it was for them, the end of the world as they knew it.

Such carnage has been seen throughout history and on vastly greater scales, but seldom has there been such a concerted effort to specifically erase all trace of what had been. The Nazis were so proud of their work, they made a film of the process.

For most of us in the modern world of today, it would take a lot less than the experience of Lidice to end the world as we know it. For some, it could be done with the removal of their mobile phone and access to social media – yes, that's how ungrateful and entitled we've become. It's typical for a generation, or at least elements of a generation, to complain about the generation that followed them. Often it's centred on the notion that things are so much easier these days: young people don't appreciate what they've got and don't appreciate how hard the generation before them worked and so on.

A typical complaint often starts along these lines, 'Young people today …' and the premise on which the complaint is based is entirely correct. However, I'm of the view no earlier generation would have fared any better than the one that followed it, or been any different than the one that followed it, had conditions been the same for both groups. People don't change, they are changed. They're changed by the conditions of their time. They're changed by the environment in which they're raised and that is why there is the appearance of so much difference.

Just to be even clearer, we are products of our environment, as much as that is a bone of contention for a lot of people, history and studies of human behaviour make that a matter of fact.

There are breakaways, there are rebels when it comes to contemporary thinking, standards and other environmental factors, but they are very much exceptions, not the rule, and it's likely their individual circumstances can be explained and categorised. Most people are pretty much the same in the way they think about the same things. There is tinkering around the edges when it comes to certain topics and hence why people vote differently. But even then, when it comes to voting, there isn't so much separation of individuals that is seen, rather, it is a separation of groups, or sides. Instead of everyone being different, we see two or three categories of opinion with almost everybody divided up between those categories. So rather than the notion of, we are all different, we are all individuals, we commonly see just two or three actual differences with almost all people subscribing to one of the two or three options and adopting that as their view. Humans like to think they're all different, all individuals, but human behaviour would seem to point to the opposite.

I can't help but think of the *Monty Python's Life of Brian*, where Brian, who has been wrongly identified as the Messiah, is trying to dissuade people from following and worshipping him. Brian says, 'You don't need to follow anybody. You've got to think for yourselves. You're all individuals.'

Then the crowd responds in unison, 'Yes we're all individuals.'

Brian says, 'You're all different.'

Then the crowd responds in unison, 'Yes, we are all different.'

Though one more self-aware member of the crowd says, 'I'm not.' But he is shushed by everyone.

Even those who might differ noticeably by identifying against the group thinking or expression are mostly kept in check by majority numbers. People like to see themselves as different, but there doesn't really seem to be much difference, let alone the crazy notion we're all unique. Once upon a time, it is as if there was a collective embrace of sameness and people worked together, but I expect that broke down most noticeably as tribes became larger groups and social factions formed.

It's clearly necessary for invention and progress that there must be independent thinking. We need those who think outside the square, as they say, and human society has benefitted from those free-thinkers. Equally, however, is the need for the close continuation of collective thinking – the group must determine rules and live by those rules in a fashion that protects the whole without impeding advancement.

It's a tricky state of affairs easily corrupted and derailed by allowing too much of what we today call 'freedoms'. Yeah, sorry about that – I have actually identified, 'freedoms', at least when in excess, to be a problem, indeed, such a problem as to contribute significantly to the fall of society.

For me, there is a question mark as to the overall life that has been built by western democracies/societies. There is a lot to be said for the simpler life, such as that which would have been seen in an extended-family-type village, but I am by no means saying that is anywhere near ideal. Equally, we can rightfully more than rave about the extraordinary advantages of modern twenty-first century society with its technological marvels, breakthrough medical miracles and lists of apparent achievements of which there are too many to note.

As is often the case in the answer to most complex questions, a mix of varied input and direction usually provides the best path. It'll never be perfect, because perfect outcomes cannot be produced by imperfect beings, who also represent so many competing interests.

Another inherent problem is that, as a species, our emotional evolution hasn't anywhere near kept pace with technological advances. In many respects, it's questionable as to whether we can handle the future we're developing.

I started out with 'the end is nigh', as in many ways that has been true in the minds of the generations who preceded us, because the world changed to such a degree, as to almost seem alien. That is true even for me; the world isn't as it was for me, and I am deeply worried for what I see ahead. I acknowledge my parents and grandparents felt the same, yet we're all still here. In fact, there are more of us here now than ever before, despite devastating diseases, wars, famine, genocide. The human race just keeps on keeping on. Despite what we do oh so negatively to virtually every other species of creature and the planet itself, we're here and there's more of us every day. Just that on its own is unsustainable.

I would never suggest I am an environmentalist as such and I won't tell you climate change will destroy the planet. By the way, it's 'the' planet, not 'our' planet – we just live here, we don't own it. We've merely become organised and militant enough to displace the claims of all other creatures.

Oh, by the way, in case you're wondering, it is still David Oldfield writing this – I note that, because depending on where you're up to in this book, much of what I'm saying here will be way off anything you expect from me.

Humans have lost their place, and along the way, we've displaced everything else, and do so more and more every day. I won't for a second pretend this is new, but we will, without question, be our own undoing, and where once I may have thought that could be avoided, I no longer believe that to be possible. However you might like to determine the means or the various means by which it will come about, the world as we know it will end. I don't mean like it did for our parents and grandparents, I mean actually and more seriously end.

Now, if you haven't already closed this book, let me assure you, I don't have a Mayan calendar or some thoughts from Nostradamus or any such nonsense. All I have is my view of an ever-growing population of over catered to selfish people heading down a funnel where there isn't going to be enough of an opening at the other end for everyone to get through.

Albert Einstein is quoted as saying, 'I know not with what weapons World War III will be fought, but World War IV will be fought with sticks and stones.'

It's suggested Einstein was a troubled man (who of us isn't?) and I'd put to you his statement isn't at all correct and wasn't meant to be as it seems. It's most likely an expression of the devastation the weapons of WW III would wreak, the result being that humans would be returned to the Stone Age. Einstein's position was an understandable one given the nuclear weapons used on Hiroshima and Nagasaki to finally bring WW II to its end.

It's more than seventy years on from Einstein's musings and we can be fairly certain that regardless of how the end, as we know it, might come – pandemic, nuclear arsenals, crop failures – people and weapons other than sticks and stones will survive. It may even be something entirely beyond our control that we had no way to avoid that gets us before we get ourselves, but then it'll be our reaction to the world that's left that will finish us off.

The real questions are, how many people will survive, where will they be, and what will life be like from then on? The answers to all of these are dependent on what exactly takes us out.

Of course, it won't be just one thing. It may start as one thing, but wherever there is chaos, whatever the cause, there are accompanying shortages and generally disease. Even once the initial issues are resolved, there'll be the aftermath of civil unrest and overall social breakdown with few if any countries untouched. Even those countries considered out of the way will eventually be impacted by the pressures placed on them by survivors from elsewhere. Places lucky enough to be seemingly untouched will suffer from countless millions seeking safe haven and many more will die as a consequence even though the initial cause of the dilemma may be long past.

Think you've seen closed borders? You have no idea of the desperation, fear and hatred that will meet refugees from the end of the world. No matter how it starts or who starts it, no-one will be completely removed from the impact, and indeed, life as we know it, really will come to an end. For a while, elements of the human race may go back to a village-style existence – small communities, that as history shows us will ultimately grow, just as they did before.

As to WW IV and Einstein's sticks and stones, the weapons used therein will be determined by how long it takes the world to recover to a point where the human desire for dominance brings it all on again, but it won't be sticks and stones.

The most frustrating aspect is that I wouldn't, by any stretch, be on my own in thinking this to be a certainty, but there'll still be no avoiding it. Humans have written the script for their own future and despite the very unhappy ending, there'll be no changes to the plan. That, is who we are!

The end is nigh – human behaviour points to it just being a matter of time.

Acknowledgements

As is always the case at my time in life, there are many people I should note, but room precludes me from getting to them all.

This book is about how I really am and gives insights as to how that came to be so it's appropriate to start by thanking all those who have judged me fairly and known me well enough to do that. A few of them have kindly provided contributions to this book, and I'm very appreciative of what they had to say.

I'd like to thank my wife Lisa for her help and patience, except she wasn't much help and she's never been patient. She did however give me my beautiful sons, so I remain grateful for that.

To my sons, I thank you for forcing me to become a responsible adult, though I acknowledge I'm still working on being the dad you deserve. I love you both more than anything.

To the people who've supported me politically and otherwise and those who hate me: in your own ways, you've contributed to keeping me speaking out when I perhaps would have been better off shutting up.

To my publisher, Fiona Schultz and representative, Stephen Moriarty, thank you for arranging for me to write this book. It has been an experience that has often been therapeutic and, indeed, it reminded me of so many things I'd done.

To my editor, Liz Hardy, you had many words to pour through and pieced it all together remarkably well.

To Scott Korman, IT guru and friend, being the luddite I am, you made lots of things easier than I could've ever done myself – much appreciated.

My apologies to anyone I have genuinely wronged thus far in my life. I'm not a bad person, but at times I've been hellishly selfish and unthinking.

To the amazing animals with whom I've shared my life, thank you for making me appreciate that humans aren't anywhere near as important as they think themselves to be. My horses, my dogs, my parrots and all the others I interact with daily, I'm lucky to have you and love every minute I'm with you.

To my parents, Bill and June, what I've written of you and what you've done for me is laid out in this book more clearly than would be covered by a few words here, but thank you Dad and Mum – you are greatly loved and terribly missed. You continue to inspire me and give me courage and I will see to it that your grandsons master the lessons you're still teaching me.